'Gavin Reid provides a wealt
and teachers, blending a
pragmatic advice, lists of resources and wisdom based on many years
of wide experience in the field.'

— *Professor Steve Chinn, PhD, FRSA*

'Gavin Reid has provided a much-needed text which will greatly
assist practitioners in the timely identification and educational support
planning for dyslexia. The clear emphases upon partnership working
with parents and children's motivation are particularly relevant for the
early years practitioner. With its authoritative, practical and accessible
style, this book will be an invaluable resource for early years and
special needs practitioners.'

— *Kevin Woods, Professor of Educational and Child*
Psychology, University of Manchester, UK

'An excellent resource! Dr Reid holds a unique ability to provide
practical and necessary information with an international perspective.
Beyond the first read, this book holds valuable resources for reference
again and again. *Dyslexia in the Early Years* is a must-read for parents,
educators and those who support children with dyslexia.'

— *Corey Zylstra, MEd, International OG/MSL Teacher Trainer and*
Executive Director of REACH OG Learning Centres, Canada

'It has been a very great pleasure to read and recommend Gavin
Reid's new book, *Dyslexia in the Early Years*, a resource that should
prove invaluable to teachers, researchers and parents. Gavin has a
unique ability to smoothly incorporate the latest developments in both
theory and practice into an approachable format for his readers, while
successfully addressing some of the current controversies. A range
of resources are highlighted for teachers to meet the individual and
classroom needs of this age group, not only in literacy skills but also
in the important wider aspects of learning, including both social and
emotional well-being.'

— *Emeritus Professor Angela Fawcett*

PreA- research - p31 Vellutino, 2004
Dyslexia signs vlot- 59
0-6 p64

of related interest

Can I Tell You about Dyslexia?
A Guide for Friends, Family and Professionals
Alan M. Hultquist
Illustrated by Bill Tulp
ISBN 978 1 84905 952 7
eISBN 978 0 85700 810 7

An Introduction to Dyslexia for Parents and Professionals
Alan M. Hultquist
ISBN 978 1 84310 833 7
eISBN 978 1 84642 527 1
JKP Essentials Series

Specific Learning Difficulties
What Teachers Need to Know
Diana Hudson
Illustrated by Jon English
ISBN 978 1 84905 590 1
eISBN 978 1 78450 046 7

Dyslexia Advocate!
How to Advocate for a Child with Dyslexia within the Public Education System
Kelli Sandman-Hurley
ISBN 978 1 84905 737 0
eISBN 978 1 78450 274 4

RISE
add 'reflective practice
p55

Retell p58

Dyslexia
IN THE
Early Years

A Handbook for Practice

GAVIN REID

Jessica Kingsley *Publishers*
London and Philadelphia

First published in 2017
by Jessica Kingsley Publishers
73 Collier Street
London N1 9BE, UK
and
400 Market Street, Suite 400
Philadelphia, PA 19106, USA

www.jkp.com

Library of Congress Cataloging in Publication Data
Names: Reid, Gavin, author.
Title: Dyslexia in the early years : a handbook for practice / Gavin Reid.
Description: Philadelphia : Jessica Kingsley Publishers, 2017. | Includes
    bibliographical references and index.
Identifiers: LCCN 2016039575 (print) | LCCN 2016058402 (ebook) | ISBN
    9781785920653 (alk. paper) | ISBN 9781784503277 (ebook)
Subjects: LCSH: Dyslexic children--Education (Early childhood)--Handbooks,
    manuals, etc. | Dyslexia--Treatment.
Classification: LCC LC4708 .R4525 2017 (print) | LCC LC4708 (ebook) | DDC
    371.91/44--dc23

British Library Cataloguing in Publication Data
A CIP catalogue record for this book is available from the British Library

ISBN 978 1 78592 065 3
eISBN 978 1 78450 327 7

Printed and bound in the United States

Contents

Acknowledgements

When writing a book such as this the most important factor for the author is support and encouragement – although advice is always welcome too, of course. In this respect I wish to acknowledge friends and colleagues who, perhaps without knowing it, have contributed to this book. Dr Jennie Guise from Dysguise Ltd is a continual source of support and encouragement along with her husband Nick, who is also very experienced in this field. Dr Sionah Lannen has been a close confidante for all my professional life, and as an educational psychologist and former teacher she has provided sound advice, as has her husband Colin, Principal of the Red Rose School for children with specific learning difficulties and coordinator of a major European project in specific learning difficulties.

Many others have contributed in some way, and I would like to offer grateful thanks to all of them – in Canada, Corey Zylstra from REACH Learning Centre and Jenn Clark, an Orton-Gillingham tutor at the Centre; good friends from SPELD New Zealand and SPELD Australia and the Learning Difference Convention; Mandy Appleyard from the Fun Track Learning Centre in Perth, Western Australia; Angela Fawcett, who wears many hats in many countries; friends and colleagues in Kuwait and Dubai, Gad Elbeheri, John Everatt and Jo Page; and closer to home, colleagues at the Helen Arkell Dyslexia Centre and the British Dyslexia Association and, of course, Dyslexia Scotland!

Such support and encouragement is essential for any author in this field, and professional and personal collaboration greatly helps to maintain motivation and progression. They have all contributed in some way to shaping this book, and I offer grateful thanks for this.

Preface

I have been involved in the field of dyslexia for many years – in teaching, assessment, teacher training and research – and I have always believed that the early years stage is the most crucial of all the education stages. It is in early years that the foundations for learning are laid, and where any potential difficulties can be identified. The early years stage for the purposes of this book is approximately from ages 3–7. Reference will be made to children younger and slightly older, but the focus is on nursery and early years.

In the case of dyslexia the research has always been convincing that early identification is the key – and this leads to early intervention. It is this early intervention that holds the promise of eventual success, and that also leads to monitoring, meaning that no child with dyslexic-type difficulties should be missed. All too often now I have come across students in secondary and higher education who had only *then* been identified. Many had gone through the whole of their schooling undetected, and although in many cases they had met some successes, they were always quick to point out the challenges that confronted them. Of course how they dealt with those challenges did stand them in good stead and helped them develop more effective learning techniques, but this was at a cost. That cost was often in terms of increasing pressure of time as invariably they required more time to study and to complete work, and exam results were usually lower because they had to rush through work. Although the education system has now moved on in terms of exam accommodations and now considers assessment based on the student's class work, there is still a need for a diagnosis, and that can often lead to further support.

It should be clear therefore that early intervention is crucial and can lead to supports being put in place at the appropriate time.

The rationale behind this book therefore is to ensure that the text is accessible to all teachers irrespective of their current understanding of dyslexia. This is important as teachers are in the best position to spot difficulties as soon as they arise, and with knowledge and understanding of dyslexia they will be able to identify those children who are at risk of dyslexia and therefore at risk of failing. The aim is to prevent failure! If failure gets a hold too early, this can lead to 'learned helplessness' and ultimately disaffection with school. This situation should never occur!

Much has been done in this area with UK government initiatives such as the landmark report from a panel led by Sir Jim Rose, the *Independent Review of the Teaching of Early Reading* (Rose 2006), the *Early Years: Guide to the 0 to 25 SEND Code of Practice* (DfE 2014) and reports from other organisations such as *Guidance for Identifying and Supporting Young Children with Special Educational Needs for Early Years Settings, Schools and Support Services* (Sure Start Children's Centres 2010) and in Scotland the *Early Years Framework* (The Scottish Government 2008) and the *National Practice Guidance on Early Learning and Childcare* (The Scottish Government 2014). In July 2016 the Scottish government announced that local authorities are to offer new patterns of early learning and childcare to provide more flexibility for families. The Scottish Minister for Childcare and Early Years, Mark McDonald, stated that the early years are a crucial time in a child's development, and evidence has shown access to high-quality early learning and childcare helps improve educational outcomes (see, for example, Pickering 2016).

The area of early years is therefore seen as one that warrants considerable support and extended provision and this, coupled with the drive by expanding networks such as the British Dyslexia Association (BDA), Dyslexia Action and the Helen Arkell Dyslexia Centre, and government initiatives such as the Rose reports (2006, 2009), and the UK government's pledge to specialist funding for teacher training in dyslexia, presents a promising picture.

In the United States the Response to Intervention (RTI) model is now used extensively. The RTI approach focuses on the provision of effective reading instruction in the pre-school and 1st grade classroom. Progress monitoring is carried out and additional help (e.g., small group-based tutoring) is provided after documenting a failure to respond to effective instruction in the regular classroom. A hybrid model of identification that combines elements of the traditional and RTI approaches through identifying measures of phonological processing and rapid naming can be used with children who are non-responders in an RTI model. The key point is that the need to identify reading difficulties early has been established!

Many other countries are considering this approach, and becoming aware of its merits. While it is an important time for all children, for those with potential dyslexic difficulties, the importance of this stage in education cannot be underplayed. Some countries have a prominent approach for early intervention – for example, in Canada the Orton-Gillingham (OG) approach is well established (see Chapter 4).

We are fortunate in having at our disposal a huge array of exciting and innovative activities for the early years. These are well documented throughout this book, and technology is at the forefront. This is also described in detail in this book, in addition to how materials can be accessed and developed.

It is a pleasure for me to be writing this book. I have always promoted effective learning, and feel that helping children become better and more effective learners is of paramount importance. And for children with dyslexia, this is vital – they need to become confident and independent learners to overcome the challenges of dyslexia. It is important, however, that there is government and school management commitment to ensuring that children at risk of dyslexia are identified and that appropriate next steps are established. Identification and support in the early years can help pave the way for this, and I sincerely hope this book helps to do this in some way.

Dr Gavin Reid
Edinburgh, Scotland, August 2016

Ages and Stages:
Early Years and Primary

Age	Year/Stage (by country)				
	England	Scotland	Northern Ireland	US/Canada	Australia
4–5	Reception/ Early Years	Primary 1	P1	Pre-Kindergarten	Pre-school
5–6	Year 1/ Key Stage 1	Primary 2	P2	Kindergarten	Reception/ Foundation Year
6–7	Year 2/ Key Stage 1	Primary 3	P3	First grade	Grade/ Year 1
7–8	Year 3/ Key Stage 2	Primary 4	P4	Second grade	Grade/ Year 2
8–9	Year 4/ Key Stage 2	Primary 5	P5	Third grade	Grade/ Year 3
9–10	Year 5/ Key Stage 2	Primary 6	P6	Fourth grade	Grade/ Year 4
10–11	Year 6/ Key Stage 2	Primary 7	P7	Fifth grade	Grade/ Year 5

Chapter 1

Dyslexia, Pre-school and the Early Years
The Context

Dyslexia is a term that is increasingly referred to but not always understood. It is often only through experience as a teacher, or a parent, that one can fully appreciate the nature and impact of dyslexia. Dyslexia can have a major impact on the child and also on the family. For that reason liaison and communication between home and school is extremely important, particularly in the early years.

It is also important to acknowledge that this impact may not always be negative – indeed, it can have a *positive impact*. Finding out exactly what the issues are can be a positive experience, and noting the skills displayed by children who are dyslexic can also have a positive impact on all. For some families knowledge of what they are up against can be a vital piece of information. Similarly the term 'dyslexia' can also provide an explanation for the parents and teacher on the best type of approach for the young child. Generally the earlier the better, but any early screening or assessment needs to be carried out by a suitably professional and qualified person.

For young children, though, early recognition of dyslexia can be tricky. Although there are criteria and characteristics of dyslexia, it is not always easy to pinpoint these and obtain a sufficient cluster of characteristics that can warrant a diagnosis. It is hoped that the following chapters, and Chapter 2 in particular, will develop this point and display some clarity in relation to this so that dyslexia can be formally identified at a very early stage.

There can be variations in the degree and type of challenges children with dyslexia experience, and much depends on the learning environment and stage of education as well as the child's cognitive and learning skills.

Defining dyslexia

The Rose Review (2009, p.11) provided the following definition of dyslexia:

> A learning difficulty primarily affecting skills involved in accurate and fluent word reading and spelling. The main characteristics are difficulties in phonological processing, verbal memory and verbal processing speed. Dyslexia occurs across the range of intellectual abilities. It is best thought of as a continuum not a distinct category and there are no clear cut-off points.

The Scottish Government (no date) provided the following definition through a cross-party working group in the Scottish Parliament:

> Dyslexia can be described as a continuum of difficulties in learning to read, write and/or spell, which persist despite the provision of appropriate learning opportunities. These difficulties often do not reflect an individual's cognitive abilities and may not be typical of performance in other areas.

The impact of dyslexia as a barrier to learning varies in degree according to the learning and teaching environment, as there are often associated difficulties, such as:

- auditory and/or visual processing of language-based information

- phonological awareness

- oral language skills and reading fluency

- short-term and working memory

- sequencing and directionality

- number skills

- organisational ability.

Motor skills and coordination may also be affected.

Dyslexia exists in all cultures and across the range of abilities and socio-economic backgrounds. It is a hereditary, lifelong, neurodevelopmental condition. Unidentified, it is likely to result in low self-esteem, high stress, atypical behaviour and low achievement:

> Learners with dyslexia will benefit from early identification, appropriate intervention and targeted effective teaching, enabling them to become successful learners, confident individuals, effective contributors and responsible citizens. (The Scottish Government no date)

Reid (2016a) suggests the following:

> Dyslexia is a term that is used to describe people who usually have a difficulty with reading, writing and/or spelling. Usually the person is around average intelligence and in some cases can be well above.
>
> It is useful to look at dyslexia as being a learning difference rather than a learning difficulty. This is because many people with dyslexia are able to make significant progress academically and excel in careers too if the opportunities are present for them to use their own particular learning preferences. Usually they are visual and experiential learners and find learning though listening and reading lengthy texts quite demanding.
>
> The key to progress is to ensure that learning materials are presented in a multisensory way that is using all modalities particularly the visual and the tactile. In this way they will be able to use their strengths and this is important if they are going to be able to develop independent and successful strategies.
>
> People with dyslexia can also have other characteristics in addition to difficulties with literacy. They may have difficulties with processing speed, short term and long term memory and sequencing and ordering information. They may also have difficulties with structuring and organising written work.
>
> Often they may not display their full abilities in written tests and if they get the opportunity to do some of it orally they usually score higher grades.

In summary, this means that:

- Dyslexia is a *processing difference* characterised by difficulties in literacy.

- It can affect *cognition* such as memory, speed of processing, time management, coordination and directional aspects.

- There can be *visual and phonological* difficulties.

- It is important that the *individual differences* and learning styles are acknowledged.

- It is also important to acknowledge the learning *contexts*.

This last point is important as the learning context can be controlled and adapted. Some features of the early years classroom environment that can have an impact on the progress of those at risk of dyslexia are discussed later in this chapter.

There can be variations in the degree and type of challenges children with dyslexia experience, and much depends on the learning environment and stage of education as well as the child's cognitive and learning skills.

Pre-school and early years of education are crucially important for any aspect of learning and for overall cognitive development – this is a well-understood and accepted view. It is also accepted that early identification of any difficulties including dyslexia is vital at this stage. Yet, while it can be quite difficult to diagnose and identify children who are at risk of dyslexia at this stage, *this must be done*, and children who are displaying some characteristics that can be associated with dyslexia, however mild, must be flagged up and followed through.

This chapter highlights some of the key aspects of pre-school and early years education and what the impact of these can be for those suspected of having dyslexia. Subsequent chapters look in detail at key factors such as assessment, diagnosis and intervention.

This introductory chapter therefore sets the scene for the book by highlighting key aspects of the nursery and early years classroom. Particular attention is paid to specific tasks and trigger points in various aspects of learning and different activities, some of which can be demanding for children at risk of dyslexia.

Early Years Foundation Stage

In England the statutory framework for the Early Years Foundation Stage (EYFS) should be a helpful guide to schools. It addresses the learning environment, partnerships with parents, learning foundations and quality of provision (DfE 2014a). The framework, which focuses on children up to 5 years old, indicates that for literacy children should be encouraged to link sounds and letters and to begin to read and write. It is highly likely that children with potential dyslexia will stand out even at this stage as they will be lagging behind, and this should be noted in the assessment that accompanies the EYFS. In many countries most 5-year-olds are eager to read and are readily absorbed in books, which is not the case for the learner with dyslexia, and this can be a key point to observe. As we will discuss later, observation is an important aspect of early identification.

The EYFS framework identifies three key areas:

- communication and language

- physical development

- personal, social and emotional development.

Children with dyslexia can have difficulties in communication and language and personal, social and emotional development. Communication and language is the most obvious area, and this can easily be detected at pre-school and early years. They may also show social and emotional issues, but it is likely these will not reveal themselves until later, when they become more aware of the gap between their performance and their peers' gradually widening. A positive emotional wellbeing needs to be developed before this happens, and before such differences have a negative impact. One way of doing this is to ensure that learning is not exclusively dependent on reading and writing. Difficulties in literacy should not prevent children from developing learning skills, and the experience of being a learner should be exciting for all at the early stages, so literacy skills should not in any way deter children from enjoying the learning experience.

Factors that can prompt concern at pre-school and school age

Pre-school

Concern may be raised in a pre-school child if some of the following are present:

- *Forgetfulness:* This is more than the occasional instance of forgetfulness, but something that is obvious most of the time.

- *Speech difficulty:* This in itself does not necessarily mean the child has dyslexia, but quite often at this stage children with dyslexia may have difficulty with certain sounds and the pronunciation of certain words. O'Keefe and Farrugia (2016) list a number of criteria for identifying children with speech and language difficulties, and quite a number of these overlap with dyslexia. For example:

  » being off-task

  » not able to follow instructions

  » has a poor discrimination of sounds

  » copies peers

  » continuously asks for help

  » has difficulty understanding the meanings of concepts such as 'more/less', 'same/different' or 'before/after'

  » uses the wrong word

  » has sequencing difficulties.

- *Reversing letters/numbers:* This is often seen as the main sign of dyslexia in young children, but it can be very misleading. Most children at some point will reverse letters or numbers. The child with dyslexia may do this more regularly, but this one factor in itself is not necessarily a sign of dyslexia – some children who are dyslexic may never reverse letters or numbers. Perhaps too much emphasis has been placed on this particular characteristic.

- *Difficulty remembering letters of the alphabet:* This is very often noted in young children with dyslexia. Not only does this

tempest

require memory skills, but it also requires skills in sequencing, and this can be a real challenge for young children with dyslexia.

- *History of dyslexia in the family:* This is becoming increasingly important as more and more is being discovered about the importance and reality of hereditary influences in dyslexia. Molfese *et al.* (2008) indicate that there is a large body of research on children at risk due to family history of dyslexia, citing seven longitudinal studies covering age ranges from pre-school/kindergarten through 2nd, 4th or 6th grade. The studies include measures of cognitive skills obtained from children as well as measures of later reading skills, and include a comparison/control group. Molfese *et al.* argue that it is more difficult to identify children with dyslexia before reading age, but that measures of brain processing of speech sounds by pre-school children and their behavioural performance on measures of letter identification provide evidence for the influence of familial risk in dyslexia. This can be conducted prior to reading age.

- *Coordination difficulties (e.g., bumping into tables and chairs):* Not all children with dyslexia will have coordination difficulties – in fact, this could involve a minority of children – but it is something to look out for and is fairly easy to spot (see also Chapter 2).

- *Difficulty with tasks that require fine motor skills (such as tying shoelaces):* This can be quite common among children with dyslexia, and they may have difficulties with other fine motor activities such as colouring in pictures and tracing.

- *Slow at reacting to some tasks:* Processing speed is often one of the cognitive factors associated with dyslexia and this can be noted in terms of reaction time as well as the time taken to carry out a task. This tends to be one of the persistent indicators of dyslexia and can be noted all the way through school.

- *Confusing words that sound similar:* It is widely accepted that 'sound discrimination' is a factor in dyslexia and can be noted particularly with younger children.

- *Losing and misplacing items:* Many children do this, but this can be a feature of dyslexia all the way through school. It can be particularly noted in secondary school where the student has to remember quite a number of different items for different subjects. It may also be a factor in other stages too, such as pre-school and the early stages of education.

School age

If some of the following characteristics are present at school age, concern may be raised:

- *Reluctance to go to school:* This can be a sign that all is not well for whatever reason. It may be because the young child is experiencing many difficulties in the work the class are doing. This needs to be investigated before it becomes the main problem!

- *Signs of not enjoying school:* This can also be a factor that needs to be investigated – in this case it is best to find out what the child does enjoy and to try to highlight and develop that activity. If the child is not enjoying reading, for example, this needs to be investigated further.

- *Reluctance to read:* Most very young children like books, even though they may not be able to read them. If they are reluctant to read, this may be a sign that they are experiencing difficulties with reading and this needs to be investigated further (see Chapter 2).

- *Difficulty decoding words:* This involves difficulty learning words and letters as well as with phonics (sounds). This means that when the child comes across a word he or she has not seen before, they find it difficult to decode it as they have little effective 'word attack' skills. These are important for reading, as it is very likely that they will come across new words. Even words they already know may have to be decoded as they may not have automaticity in reading the word. Practise in decoding new words using phonic rules and onset and rime (i.e., identifying the beginning and end of a word) is very important for decoding.

- *Poor memory:* This is often a sign of dyslexia, although it doesn't affect all children with dyslexia. Memory comprises *[short-term]* of short-term memory (this can be half a second), working *[term]* memory (remembering two or more factors at the same time *[working]* or remembering something and carrying out an activity at the same time, such as saying numbers backwards) and long-term *[long-term]* memory (which also involves the recall of information when required). Children with dyslexia may know the information but are not able to recall it without prompts. The key thing for the teacher is to identify which prompts are the most effective! *[*]*

- *Coordination difficulties:* These can have a major impact on self-esteem as the child develops and becomes more aware of his or her difficulties and is able to compare his or her performance with others.

- *Handwriting difficulties:* This is also often a factor to consider. The child may have difficulty forming letters or numbers and also difficulty in copying or in colouring in pictures.

- *Poor organisation of materials:* This is usually a feature that can be noted further up the school year but it is worth mentioning here too. Often children will have a lot of materials to work with at any one time, and they often need to be arranged and organised. Difficulty with organisation is seen as an issue for children with dyslexia.

After around two years at school

These points normally become more obvious after around two years of schooling, and include:

- hesitancy in reading

- poor 'word attack' skills

- poor knowledge of sounds and words

- difficulty recognising where in words particular sounds come from

- substitution of words when reading (e.g., bus for car).

Additionally, spelling difficulties can begin to be noted here too, and we should be looking for persistent spelling errors or indeed inconsistency in spelling (discussed later in this book).

In summary, some general factors that can impact on learning for young people with dyslexia include:

- listening to instructions

- following the sequence in a story

- measuring quantities, for example, in the sand tray

- remembering the routines of the class

- motivation

- concentration

- handwriting.

Cross-linguistic factors

Multicultural and multilinguistic classrooms are now the norm, and so it can be quite easy to use bilingualism as a reason for a child not progressing in English. While this may be the case in some instances, it is unlikely to be the main reason for a reading difficulty – the child who is bilingual will also experience difficulties in his or her home language as well as in English.

Mahfoudhi, Elbeheri and Everatt (2009) found that, as in English, differences in phoneme and syllable structure between spoken and written Arabic have been found to interfere with performance on phonemic awareness and pseudo-word reading tasks among pre-school and 1st grade learners.

While Palti (2016) indicates that bilingualism is an additional risk factor for dyslexic children, she argues that research has shown that the same cognitive inefficiencies count for, or help identify, dyslexia in the first and second languages. Among these are phonological awareness and processing, fluency and retrieval speeds, and short-term and working memory skills. Given that similar cognitive processes apply across languages, the provision for supporting dyslexic pupils in the main language could also be applied to the second language, as knowledge is transferable between the languages.

Geva and Herbert (2012) suggest that, in general terms, pupils who have decoding and spelling problems in their first language also have difficulties in their second language. Phonological awareness, rapid naming, and to some extent verbal working memory, are sources of individual differences that are associated with reading development and difficulties in both languages, regardless of whether these skills are measured in children in their first or second language, and whether the language is alphabetic or non-alphabetic. This suggests that the same underlying cognitive and linguistic component skills that are crucial for learning literacy skills in monolingual or first language pupils (e.g., phonemic awareness, speed of processing, visual processes) contribute across diverse languages and writing systems. This also means that these skills influence the development of literacy skills in the second language and bilingual pupils.

Features of the early years environment

The classroom environment should be seen in a flexible and non-restrictive manner. This means more than re-positioning desks and chairs; it relates to broader educational practices, such as physical layout, the facilitation of social interaction and how conducive the environment is to teaching and learning.

Reid (2007) suggests that environmental features can lead to environmental preferences. This helps the learner – even the very young learner – acquire more self-awareness and self-knowledge within the learning paradigm. Some factors that are important to consider include:

- *Organisation:* This should focus on how learners organise themselves in terms of their cognitive organisation, as well as the materials they need to use. Cognitive organisation refers to:

  » *Input:* How information is initially processed and remembered in short-term memory.

  » *Cognition:* How the information is understood, organised and retained for future use.

  » *Output:* How the information is presented by the child to show the degree of mastery achieved.

In each of these cognitive stages the child is required to organise the information he or she is processing. Some children find this quite demanding. Making observations as they are going through these processes can provide insights into their learning preferences, and this can have implications for the learning environment. (These points are discussed in later chapters.)

- *Attention:* It is important to assess the types of tasks that can promote, or indeed distract, the child. These can be seen by noting the environment and the types of tasks that can maintain and extend the learner's attention. It is quite important to recognise when the child's attention wavers and to note the tasks he or she was undertaking at that time.

- *Sequencing:* It is also useful to note how the child sequences information. This can give an indication in relation to their learning style and how the task should be presented for them. For example, does the child prefer information in neat columns or numbers, or does he or she prefer to learn in a more random manner?

- *Interaction:* A great deal of information can be gleaned from the type of interaction children engage in, and some environments can be more conducive to interaction than others. For example, if the child's style is one that relies on interaction, then the environment should permit a degree of freedom to allow interaction.

- *Self-concept:* The outcome of any learning activity can be determined to a great extent by the level of the child's self-concept. Great effort needs to be made to ensure that the child feels comfortable in the environment; otherwise this may affect his or her self-concept.

- *Learning preferences:* It is important to profile the child's learning preferences. When this is done it is also essential to consider the impact of the learning environment on the child. This can be done with young children by showing them pictures and explaining different learning environments or demonstrating them and noting the child's response.

- *Motivation/initiative:* The nature and degree of motivation shown by the learning is important in determining the learning outcome. It should be noted whether this motivation stems from the learner's own initiative or whether the child needs to be prompted. This can have implications for the actual learning programme and the type of rewards, whether intrinsic or extrinsic (see later in the book).

- *Independent learning:* Ideally this is what all children should be striving for. Some can achieve this quite readily, while others need a significant amount of support and structure. It is important to determine this so that a structure can be developed if necessary. It is also important to consider how structures can be gradually removed. It can be quite difficult to determine the balance between structuring and removing support.

These factors can be applied to all children, but the responses and pattern of responses can have implications for the teaching and learning of children, either with dyslexia or at high risk of dyslexia.

The role of early identification

This will be discussed in detail in the next chapter, but this point is picked up in almost every government, local authority or voluntary organisation document regarding the early years. For example, Oxfordshire County Council's *Guidance for Identifying and Supporting Young Children with Special Educational Needs for Early Years Settings, Schools and Support Services* (Sure Start Children's Centres 2010) gives a key role to observation, assessment and planning for the optimum learning environment for children with any form of special needs. It says that 'through observing each child's achievements and interests... practitioners can respond through their interactions with new activities or changes to the environment in ways to help children learn' (2010, p.3). The guidance indicates that before action is taken following observations and assessment, the following must be taken into account:

- The child has received learning opportunities that are adapted to the way the child learns.

- Adjustments have been made for the child within the normal day-to-day organisation of the setting.

- The child's responses to opportunities have been observed and recorded.

All these points are important and each can apply to identifying children at risk of dyslexia. In fact, it is crucial at this stage to ensure these points have been implemented before taking the assessment process one stage further.

Steps to intervention

An important point the Oxfordshire County Council document makes in the section on supporting the child's learning is 'to break down skills and activities into smaller achievable steps' (Sure Start Children's Centres 2010 p.17). This is important for those children at risk of dyslexia, because most children will be reading spontaneously, but children with dyslexia will not, and they will almost immediately realise this. In order to prevent 'learned helplessness',[1] it is important that the children experience some success. Breaking tasks and activities down into small manageable and achievable steps can do this, which is crucial for young children at risk of dyslexia.

In terms of intervention (discussed later in this book), a great number of programmes, strategies and activities can be used. Two that are increasingly popular are the Nessy learning materials[2] and the Jolly Phonics materials.[3] The Jolly Phonics materials focus on sound recognition, auditory training and reading schemes as well as writing and spelling, and the research evidence for their approach comes from the well-known Clackmannanshire study (Watson and Johnston 1998), which has been followed up a number of times since. The Nessy learning materials cater well for the use of technology and have a number of game ideas that can also be incorporated into an early years programme.

---

1   Learned helplessness occurs when the child experiences repeated failure and loses the motivation to try the activity as he or she anticipates failure.
2   See www.nessy.com
3   See http://jollylearning.co.uk

Crombie and Reid (2009) argue that social circumstances and factors in the home impact on young children. This includes parenting practices, family activities, the language spoken at home, exposure to books and magazines and socio-economic status (SES) variables such as parental education and occupation. Community activities also featured in the desire to heighten children's awareness of books and the need for a literacy-rich culture. Crombie and Reid go on to argue that early identification and intervention are important 'for preventing early and long-term reading difficulties in most "at risk" children', whatever the home background (2009). According to Molfese and Molfese (2002), these factors alone will not cause dyslexia, but may exacerbate it. Examples of this can be seen in the practice in one Scottish Education Authority, East Renfrewshire, where home tutors were employed to work with targeted families at pre-school stage.

Reid, Davidson-Petch and Deponio (2004), in a government-funded research project on identification and dealing with dyslexia in the early years, cite one authority that stressed a clear commitment to identifying children with specific learning difficulties as early as possible. The Pre-School Home Visiting Service is a valued resource that can be available to families from the start of child's life. Pre-school placements of children with known specific learning difficulties are then carefully planned to ensure effective support and intervention. In addition to a specialist pre-school provision for children with additional support needs there are three pre-school early intervention services that provide a range of supports to children. A key aspect of these services is to promote children's language and communication development and to identify emerging factors that may cause ongoing concern.

This is indeed a promising initiative and indicates that it can never be too early to identify literacy needs, and a home–school support and liaison system may be a valuable addition to the range of means of identifying literacy needs as early as possible.

Concluding thoughts

The aim of this chapter has been to set the scene for the book, and the following points have been established:

- The early stages of education are vitally important, and it follows that the challenges experienced by children with dyslexia need to be identified as early as possible.

- The context and learning environment are worthy of consideration as well as the individual challenges experienced by the child in relation to learning.

- Government initiatives can help to provide a framework and structure for early identification and intervention.

- Identification does not necessarily mean labelling; rather, it can be noting those children who are at 'high risk' of dyslexia.

- It is worthwhile having a list of factors that can prompt concern at different stages, including nursery and early years of primary school.

- Bilingualism is becoming the norm in most classrooms, and this can be a factor in relation to accessing literacy in English. But the research indicates that children who are bilingual and having difficulty in English are likely to be experiencing similar difficulties in their main language.

- It is a good idea to have a definition of dyslexia that is operational in the classroom, and the key points of that definition should be available to all staff.

Chapter 2

Identifying Learning Needs
Early Identification

This chapter looks at those specific areas of learning in pre-school and early years that can be challenging for children at risk of dyslexia. It therefore focuses on *observation and screening* as well as more *formal assessment* throughout the nursery and first year of schooling. There is an emphasis on *barriers to learning* and how these can be identified in the nursery setting and early years of schooling.

This chapter also considers social and emotional factors (interaction with others, that is, peer group, adults); language skills and ability to communicate; signs of tension and anxiety; and any lengthy absenteeism). Other factors that are often included in a formal assessment, such as cognition (memory), information processing and language and literacy skills, need to be considered in addition to basic numeracy and writing skills.

The educational environment is also crucial and can have a big impact on children, particularly if they are sensitive – as children who are at risk of dyslexia often are.

Factors that predict success in reading

Drysdale (2009) suggests that it is important to focus on the factors that can predict success in reading, and observing how competent children in the early years acquire these skills. She cites Wolfe (2008), who argues that to become a skilled reader, the young learner must create entirely new neurological circuitry connecting visual, auditory and motor systems at lightning speed. Development of skills within any one of these systems and the learner's ability to make neural connections at speed will affect success in learning to read. Aspects of these skills can be seen when observing children at play in the nursery and early primary stages, particularly in processing speed and auditory processing as well as motor development.

Factors that point to dyslexia

Some of the specific characteristics for dyslexia that can be taken into account include the following:

- *Memory:* Short-term memory difficulties mean difficulty remembering even simple instructions. This can also be confused with auditory processing or listening difficulties. Young children often experience a number of these kinds of difficulties, which can make diagnosis more difficult.

- *Organisation:* Although organisation is often associated with older children, it is also possible to note those children who have persistent difficulties with, for example, organising materials and any equipment they need to use for play or in the sand tray, for example.

- *Movement:* It is possible that children at risk of dyslexia will have coordination difficulties, although this is not always the case. Those who have coordination difficulties will find tying shoelaces quite difficult. Additionally they may also bump into furniture in the classroom and frequently trip over things. There is an overlap between dyslexia and dyspraxia/coordination difficulties – this means that both fine and gross motor difficulties can be experienced by both groups. Fine motor skills refer to writing, pencil grip and drawing and colouring in. Gross motor skills refer to coordination, running, jumping and skipping.

- *Speech development:* Some young children may well have speech and language difficulties and this can be their principal difficulty. Speech difficulties can often overlap with dyslexia, especially in young children with dyslexia. The difficulties include:

  » confusing similar sounds

  » poor articulation of words or sounds

> » difficulty blending sounds into words

> » poor awareness of rhymes and rhyming words

> » difficulty in naming items and remembering the names.

It is important to recognise that many of these factors can be seen in a continuum of difficulties, from mild to severe, and their extent and severity will have an impact on assessment results and subsequent recommendations for support.

What is early identification?

Early identification is twofold:

- Identifying those children who have cognitive challenges with learning and literacy.

- Monitoring and observing those children who appear resistant to intervention and as a result lag behind their peers.

It is also generally agreed that early identification is more than identifying poor readers. While this is important, concerns are raised when coming across poor readers who are resistant to intervention.

Early identification should also consider if the profile of difficulties match a potential dyslexic profile. For this, it is important to prepare a checklist with profile indicators, which can include:

- Letter and sound knowledge.

- Short-term and working memory skills.

- Alliteration and rhyming abilities (this can also be a test of articulation).

- Processing speed, which can include the naming of objects or numbers. The Phonological Assessment Battery (PhAB) test (see later in this chapter) provides a good example of naming speed using pictures.

- Sequencing information, as in a story line or how the child carries out an activity. Ulmer and Timothy (2001) developed an alternative assessment framework based on 'retelling' as an instructional and assessment tool. This indicated that informative assessment of a child's comprehension could take place by using criteria relating to how the child retells a story.

- Poor organisational skills, which can be seen at a number of levels – how the child organises materials for play, possessions and personal items used in class.

- A genetic component. This is becoming an important factor as more research becomes available on the hereditary aspects of dyslexia. Large-scale studies (Becker *et al.* 2014; Molfese *et al.* 2008; Scerri *et al.* 2010) have displayed the range of chromosomes and genes that can be implicated with dyslexia.

- Motor skills and balance difficulties can often co-occur with dyslexia, so it important to observe how the child copes with tasks such as bead threading and colouring in pictures. Also note how they cope with climbing frames and outdoor playground activities.

Checklist for high risk of dyslexia: 1. Pre-school and early years

Characteristic	Frequency	Examples	Support needed
Forgetful			
Speech difficulty			
Reversal of letters			
Difficulty remembering letters of the alphabet			
Difficulty remembering the sequence of letters of the alphabet			
Coordination difficulties			
Difficulties with fine motor skills			
Slow in completing tasks			
Poor concentration			
Reluctance to read			
Difficulty copying			
Difficulty forming letters			
Difficulty colouring			
Poor organisation of materials			

Letter tray

Checklist for high risk of dyslexia: 2. Primary school

Characteristic	Frequency	Examples	Support needed
Poor reading fluency			
Difficulty decoding new words			
Poor knowledge of the sounds of words			
Spelling difficulty			
Frustrated			
Attention and concentration difficulties			
Discrepancies between oral and written work			

Early intervention

In a longitudinal study conducted with young children in New York, Vellutino and his colleagues (Vellutino *et al.* 2004) investigated the effects of implementing early intervention for children identified on entry to kindergarten as potentially 'at risk' of reading failure. All children in the study were given a test of letter-name knowledge, and roughly 30 per cent were identified as being 'at risk for early reading difficulties' on the basis of the findings. Tests of phonological awareness (sensitivity to rhyme and alliteration), rapid automatised naming, counting by ones and number identification were also included. The 'at risk' group was given an hour's training each week during their kindergarten year, split into two sessions, from specially trained staff. The sessions, conducted in small groups of two or three children, focused on activities such as concepts of print, letter recognition, letter identification, phonological awareness, letter- Pre A
sound matching, sight word learning, shared and guided reading and listening to stories. From their results, Vellutino and his colleagues concluded that early intervention made at kindergarten stage could significantly improve early skills and prepare the children for more formal reading instruction.

All children, dyslexic or not, can benefit from a targeted focus on literacy development, so additional strategies do not need to be

small group

individual or specific to one particular child at this early stage, but should be aimed at encouraging a small group at least. The inclusion of children 'at risk' in group learning situations could bring benefits for the whole group. Although some children may not need the focused intervention, it will do no harm, and is likely to make them more confident.

Social and community factors

Young children are influenced by social circumstances and factors in the home. This includes parenting practices, family activities, language spoken at home, exposure to books and magazines and SES variables such as parental education and occupation. According to Molfese and Molfese (2002), these factors alone will not cause dyslexia, but may exacerbate it. Examples of social and community factors impacting on children were seen in the practice of one Scottish Education Authority, East Renfrewshire, where home tutors were used at the pre-school stage for targeted families. Community activities also featured in the desire to heighten children's awareness of books and the need for a literacy-rich culture (East Renfrewshire Council 1999). It is accepted, however, that early identification and intervention are important 'for preventing early and long-term reading difficulties in most "at risk" children', whatever the home background (Vellutino et al. 2004, p.7).

Follow through

Torgesen (2004a, 2004b) argues that even with appropriate intervention at an early stage, not all children will reach an age-appropriate level of reading when they proceed into the more formal learning situation. There is an ever-increasing desire to increase literacy levels, with countries easily embarrassed by international studies and 'league tables' that identify those that are failing in literacy (Shiel 2002). Substantial amounts of money and government intervention are therefore common in attempts to secure a rise in literacy levels (Reid Lyon 2004; Rose 2006). On both sides of the Atlantic, in both the US and the UK, recent studies have revealed that systematic, structured programmes for teaching reading can benefit huge numbers of children. The National Institute of Child Health and Human Development (NICHD) with the US Office of Education in the United States, and KPMG (Klynveld

Peat Marwick Goerdeler) with the University of London and the Department for Education and Skills (DfES), have both conducted research studies with large numbers of children into the effectiveness of various programmes for intervening early in a child's reading career with the lowest achieving children (Burroughs-Lange 2008; DfE and DH 2015; Gross 2006; Rose 2006; Torgesen 2005). While it is important to appreciate that reading involves a number of different skills, both decoding and comprehension of written words are vital. If children cannot decode, they are unlikely to be able to comprehend what has not been decoded. If verbal skills are weak and the children have poor vocabulary knowledge, then even teaching them to decode will not result in a high level of comprehension, so results on reading comprehension tests are likely to vary according to levels of oral understanding (Torgesen 2005).

Even when this has been taken into account, progress can be made by early intervention for the lowest achieving readers using methods such as Reading Recovery[1] and Synthetic Phonics.[2] For a very small percentage of children, those that Torgesen (2005) calls 'treatment resisters', perhaps appropriately also called 'dyslexic', more targeted and systematic multisensory programmes will be required over a longer period to achieve success. It is for these children, too, that a range of other strategies will be required to ensure that boredom through repeated use of the same material doesn't reinforce a sense of failure. While reading interventions are to be welcomed before a sense of failure becomes embedded, these potential 'treatment resisters' should be identified and targeted even earlier. If not, these children will remain vulnerable throughout their school lives.

Key factors for those at risk of dyslexia

Auditory and language skills

In a stimulating pre-school environment, most children will develop good oral language skills. Usually they will listen to stories and be able to clearly retell them in a sequence. They will start at the beginning and likely tell you the names of the characters first. The key thing is that they will be able to develop and recognise the importance of

1   See www.ucl.ac.uk/international-literacy/reading-recovery
2   See www.syntheticphonics.com/synthetic_phonics.htm

the sequence of events in the story. Children at risk of dyslexia may not see the importance of this, and will often begin at the end of the story, as that is the part they can more readily recall. The standardised test Wide Range Assessment of Memory and Learning (2nd edn) (WRAML2) (Sheslow and Adams 2003), which commences at age 5, can be used to provide information on story memory, design memory (visual), verbal learning, picture memory, as well as sentence memory and sound/symbol memory. This test can provide a considerable amount of data that can be useful for early diagnosis of dyslexia.

Rhyming

Drysdale (2009) argues that young children would normally express ideas, exchange information and ask questions; they would recognise rhyme and appreciate the humour in nonsense rhymes. Marching and singing games and clapping the syllables in each other's names will come easily to them.

While not all children will be expected to develop these skills in the same way or at the same rate, difficulties in these areas can be a pointer that something may be amiss, particularly if there is significant difficulty or delay with any of these skills.

Vocabulary

Young children are still developing a working vocabulary, but if there are signs that they are struggling, this can also be a warning point.

Certainly there is evidence that children who come to school with a broad experience of literacy and an extensive oral vocabulary have a huge advantage as beginning readers, and those whose oral vocabulary is limited are likely to find reading harder than their peers (Vellutino *et al.* 2004).

Phonological awareness

The research points to phonological awareness as the main factor associated with dyslexia, particularly in the early years. This includes being aware of and able to manipulate sounds, and able to recognise where in the word the sound is, for example, middle, beginning or end, and to recognise rhyming sounds. Children at risk of dyslexia will not be able to do this as easily.

The Phonological Assessment Battery (PhAB) test (Frederickson, Frith and Reason 1997) has a number of subtests that can be useful for assessing these types of difficulties. Although the norms for this test do not start until the age of 6, the items can give an indication of the sort of points to look for at the pre-6 level – naming speed, picture naming, digit naming and rhyming in particular would apply to a younger age group.

Identifying a profile

Early identification is more than identifying the lowest performing reading group in order to receive help, although this will increase the reading skills of many children. For many, however, it is about identifying a 'dyslexic profile' early on, using indicators such as letter and sound knowledge, short-term and working memory skills, alliteration and rhyming abilities, speedy naming of objects, sequencing, often along possible difficulties in accessing known words for objects, and possible organisation skills often along with a genetic component. While motor skills and balance difficulties often co-occur with dyslexia, they don't always, and seem to correlate to the severity of the dyslexic difficulties (Haslum and Miles 2007). With this knowledge, a protocol can be developed to ensure that we do not allow children to fail to learn without intervening to prevent that failure before it happens.

Assess, Plan, Do, Review

In England the *Special Educational Needs and Disability Code of Practice* (DfE and DH 2015) makes a strong case for early identification and intervention (Section 5.39). In terms of identifying needs, the legislation indicates that the following broad areas need to be considered for identifying specific needs: communication and interaction; cognition and learning; social, emotional and mental health; and sensory and/or physical needs (Section 5.32). The *Code of Practice* (DfE and DH 2015) applies to all English state-funded nursery, primary and secondary schools, and requires schools to work with parents on a cycle of *Assess,*

Plan, Do, Review. The expectation is that class/form teachers will meet at least termly with parents to talk through:

- What we already know/have found out.

- What we plan to do about it.

- How we will update each other on progress towards it.

- How we will know when we've achieved it.

While this process will clearly benefit children with dyslexia, it may not provide the label.

The cognition and learning factor is the one that needs to be firmly addressed in relation to dyslexia. In Scotland, an HM Inspectorate of Education report indicated very clearly the importance of identifying children's needs in pre-school, with a commitment for educational authorities to assess children who were showing signs of difficulty in learning to read or spell (2008, p.7). The idea was to tackle these difficulties before they became problematic. The beginning point for most authorities was to investigate the accuracy and fluency of their phonic skills. It was stated, however, that although identifying literacy and learning needs was a priority at this stage, there was a reluctance to actually diagnose dyslexia. While it would be useful for the label to be applied, it was not seen as essential in the very early stages, but the child should be identified as at risk of dyslexia and therefore appropriate intervention should commence and ongoing monitoring should continue (see Chapter 4).

Reid (2016a) suggests that the class teacher in the early years can identify coordination difficulties, difficulties with pencil grip, immature use of language, and sequencing or organisational difficulties, all of which can be seen prior to teaching reading skills. These can be highlighted through classroom observation, discussions with parents and diagnostic assessment.

Early identification

Early identification can and should take place despite any monitoring and review that might be ongoing. It is good practice to acknowledge if the child has dyslexia or not, and this information should be made available to parents as well as school or nursery staff.

How such identification should take place, and when it can most effectively and most sensitively be conducted, are matters of some debate (Reid 2016a). One school of thought advocates a full cognitive assessment of the child, taking into account the learning opportunities and the learning environment, while another may focus on identifying learning and literacy needs and working towards helping the child achieve competence – this would be the *Assess, Intervention, Review* model. In the US the Response to Intervention (RTI) model has this type of framework, and this involves reviewing the intervention if the child is not responding appropriately to instruction. This applies to the early years as well as further up the school.

This is an important aspect of identifying needs, however, and it is important that schools and nurseries have specific procedures in place for early identification, although not everyone agrees that children should be labelled, and many education authorities feel that identifying learning needs and putting intervention in place is sufficient.

Knight, Day and Patton-Tery (2009), from the US perspective, suggest that while it may not be desirable to diagnose and label a young child who may not be reading as dyslexic, it should be recognised that some children as young as three years of age display behaviours that indicate that they are not developing oral language, phonological awareness and motor skills as one would expect. Knight *et al.* argue that some of these children will be diagnosed with dyslexia, while others need intervention to allow them to have the necessary experiences to become readers. The point is that children in both groups are at risk for developing reading difficulties. This is the essence of early identification – not to label, but to identify those who are at risk of developing difficulties in acquiring literacy.

Knight *et al.* (2009) also provide evidence of early identification of reading difficulty along with targeted, research-based interventions improving children's chances of becoming more effective readers (Henry *et al.* 2004; Lynch 2007). This begs the questions below:

- When should early identification take place, how should it be conducted, and by whom?

- What criteria should be used at this early stage for a diagnosis?

Reid (2016a) argues that if the first of these questions is asked (When should this take place?), it is likely that the whole concept of early identification has been misunderstood. It is important to note that early identification doesn't focus exclusively on 'within-child' deficits, and these can often be apparent before the child has had an opportunity to benefit from the learning opportunities in nursery or school. Reid suggests that the term 'early identification' would be more accurate if it were extended to 'early identification of learning needs'. This would be the first stage, and once this was carried out, a formal assessment and eventual diagnosis may follow. *But it is important that after 'needs' are identified, the assessment process continues.*

Many authorities and schools use a combination of both the 'needs model' and the 'child deficit model', and it is possible to merge these two in a complementary manner. It is also important to focus on 'curriculum access' rather than 'child deficits', although any deficits in the child at this stage also need to be identified. An example of a document that includes 'curriculum access' as an integral part of the identification procedures for dyslexia is the *Report of the Task Force on Dyslexia* (Department of Education and Skills (Ireland) 2001). This document highlights the 'continuum of identification and provision', which is a policy-led identification and support model, involving the identification of students who are at risk, a review of guidance and advice, differentiated responses, regular assessment by class or learning support teachers, curriculum development to take the profile into account and implementation of the individual learning programme and monitoring of outcomes. This can be suitable for early years as well as all through the school.

Monitoring and review

If, for whatever reason, formal assessment is not possible, then close monitoring of progress is needed. In the early years, when reading skills are taught, the following should be investigated:

- The ability to discriminate words that sound the same.

- The ability to recognise and repeat sounds in words.

- Any visual difficulties, such as failure to recognise letters, comparison between visually similar letters, and missing lines when reading confusing picture cues.

- Sequencing difficulties, such as confusing the order of letters, words or digits.

- Organisational difficulties, such as directional confusion, general laterality problems and persistent left–right confusion.

- Memory – difficulty in following simple instructions.

- Coordination and general motor difficulties, for example, poor pencil grip, awkward gait, poor coordination and general clumsiness.

- Difficulty doing two simple tasks simultaneously (this should be noted, but many young children may show this behaviour).

These points are not necessarily diagnostic criteria but early warning signs, and are sufficient to be included in a monitoring programme.

The next step would be a meeting with the parents and the school/nursery management, to discuss the need for a full assessment, and if this is the case, how to proceed. It may be sufficient at this stage to review the intervention, and discussions with parents are important here. Other professionals, such as educational psychologists, occupational therapists and speech therapists, may also be consulted at this stage.

Transition

There are various transition points in a child's life when they are particularly vulnerable. Moving from the relative informality of the nursery or kindergarten to the more formal primary school years is likely to start to highlight weaknesses in literacy where these exist. Moving from one teacher to another, again with varying levels of formality of classroom organisation, can in itself cause problems, and then eventually the change from primary to secondary, where the pupils have a different format to their day but a different range of subjects, can have both positive and negative effects on the pupil.

Chapter 3

Formal Tests, Screening and Links to Intervention

Barriers to learning

It is useful to view early identification and, indeed, the assessment process, in terms of overcoming barriers to learning rather than through a child deficit focus. In reality, however, both information on the child and the curriculum are needed. Essentially, the 'overcoming barriers to learning' approach requires that all children undertake the same curriculum, irrespective of perceived abilities and difficulties. An example of this can be the way in which curriculum objectives are identified, assessing the extent to which the child has met them and what action may be needed to help him or her meet the objectives more fully. This action can take the form of some assistance for the child, but equally it can be in terms of reassessing the objectives or refining them in some way to make them more accessible.

This means that the emphasis is on the barriers that prevent the child from meeting accepted targets rather than identifying what the child cannot do. This is essentially a whole-school responsibility as it is important that attitudes relating to progress and curriculum access are consistent throughout the school. It is important that there is a consistent view throughout the school on the understanding of dyslexia, and the role of early years teachers are then crucial in identifying those children at risk of dyslexia.

Formal tests/screening procedures

Dyslexia Early Screening Test (2nd edn) (DEST-2) and Pre-school Early Screening Test (PREST)

DEST-2 contains a battery of screening tests of attainment and ability covering the age range of 4 years 6 months to 6 years 5 months (Fawcett and Nicolson 2004; Fawcett, Nicolson and Lee 2001). These determine whether a young child is experiencing difficulty in areas known to be affected in dyslexia. An 'at risk' score for dyslexia determines whether further in-depth testing should be undertaken. A profile of skills provides valuable information that can be used to guide in-school support.

The DEST-2 consists of 12 subtests:

- rapid naming
- bead threading
- phonological discrimination
- postural stability
- rhyme/alliteration
- forwards digit span
- digit naming
- letter naming
- sound order
- shape copying
- Corsi block-tapping test
- vocabulary (group/individual).

Fawcett *et al.* (2001) established that screening children in school at age 6 (using DEST-2), followed by targeted short-term intervention, could significantly assist most at risk of reading failure.

Test of Phonological Awareness (2nd edn: Plus) (TOPA-2+)

The testing time for this is 30–45 minutes for kindergarten/nursery and 15–30 minutes for early primary. This is a group-administered, norm-referenced measure of phonological awareness for children aged 5–8. The scale, which can also be administered individually, has demonstrated reliability, and the test yields valid results that are reported in terms of percentile ranks and a variety of standard scores (see Torgesen and Bryant 2004).

Comprehensive Test of Phonological Processing (2nd edn) (CTOPP-2)

CTOPP-2 assesses phonological awareness, phonological memory and rapid naming. Those with deficits in one or more of these kinds of phonological processing abilities may have more difficulty learning to read than those who do not. Individual subtests include: elision, blending words, phoneme isolation, memory for digits, non-word repetition, rapid digit naming, rapid letter naming and supplemental optional subtests on blending non-words and segmenting non-words. The testing time is 40 minutes and covers a wide age range (4 years to 24 years, 11 months), which adds to its usefulness (see Wagner *et al.* 2013).

Launch into Reading Success Through Phonological Awareness Training

This is a phonological awareness programme designed just for young children, which can prevent reading failure at an early stage if it is identified and intervention with the right programme is used. It is a phonological skills training programme designed for use by teachers and other professionals in schools and for parents at home. It can provide an effective first step for a child to take in the pursuit of literacy (see Ottley and Bennett 1997).

Dyslexia Screener

The aim of this is to diagnose pupils aged 5–16 with dyslexic characteristics through evaluation of:

- non-verbal reasoning

- phonics

- spelling

- visual search

- reading

- verbal reasoning.

As an initial diagnostic tool, it enables teachers to distinguish between poor reading ability and dyslexia, and gives advice on next steps. Standardised scores enable comparison of pupils' results to the national average (see Turner and Smith 2004).

Special Needs Assessment Profile (SNAP) Infant Check CD-ROM

This is a computer-aided assessment for use with children aged 5–7, and is designed to help pinpoint and respond immediately to potential barriers to a child's learning, at the first opportunity (see Weedon and Ruttle 2012a).

SNAP Infant Check identifies patterns of difficulties associated with the most prolific special educational needs: emergent dyslexia, dyspraxia and dyscalculia; speech, language and communication difficulties; autistic spectrum disorders; sensory impairments; and behavioural, emotional and social difficulties. It also looks beyond these core categories to analyse 15 associated strands that may contribute to a child's own unique 'mix' of difficulties.

SNAP Infant Check uses a questionnaire that draws on the teacher's professional judgement and classroom observations, with parental input if appropriate. The SNAP-I profile then links to focused activities, resources and 'next steps' advice through personalised information sheets that provide practical classroom teaching and support strategies (including home support).

It is a standalone assessment that allows the exploration of a child's patterns of difficulties, and it also profiles any apparent barriers to learning, to point the way to the most appropriate 'next steps' provision or referral, and to monitor subsequent progress.

A User's Handbook can be used with the SNAP Infant Check CD-ROM, which is available separately (Weedon and Ruttle 2012b).

Special Needs Assessment Profile (SNAP) Together Demo CD-ROM

SNAP Together combines the well-known SNAP-SpLD (Special Learning Difficulties) and SNAP-B (Behaviour) assessment profiling programmes, bringing insights to pupils' specific learning difficulties and social, emotional and behavioural difficulties in one package.

Designed for ages 5–14+, SNAP Together draws information from home and school. Carefully targeted questions identify clusters and patterns of difficulties or behaviours, and give a graphic profile that pinpoints core problem areas. For each, SNAP Together then generates information sheets that are personalised to the individual pupil, giving practical advice, information and strategies for focused and effective support, at school and at home (see Long, Weedon and Reid 2008).

Special Needs Assessment Profile – Behaviour (SNAP-B): Pupil Assessment

User-friendly, SNAP-B brings to social, emotional and behavioural difficulties the insights and practical strategies that SNAP-SpLD brings to specific learning difficulties. By identifying each pupil's core problem areas, SNAP-B enables more focused and effective support, at school and at home (see Long and Weedon 2017 [in press]).

Special Needs Assessment Profile – Special Learning Difficulties (SNAP-SpLD)

Designed for use by SENCos (special educational needs coordinators), learning support and specialist teachers in primary and secondary schools, and in SEN support services, SNAP-SpLD is a computer-aided diagnostic assessment and profiling package that brings real insights to the practical diagnosis of learning difficulties, for ages 4–16.

SNAP-SpLD gives an expanded profile for specific learning difficulties and related factors, including self-esteem. It helps to identify clusters of problems and pinpoint the core features of a pupil's difficulties. It also generates information sheets that will help to strengthen home and teacher support and point the way to the most appropriate teaching and/or specialist provision. SNAP-SpLD can also help to monitor progress and the effectiveness of intervention (see Weedon, Reid and Ruttle 2017 [in press]).

Wechsler Individual Achievement Test (2nd edn) for Teachers (WIAT-II UK-T)

WIAT-II UK-T assesses single word reading, reading comprehension, reading speed and spelling in one assessment. The age range is from 4 upwards, and this can be very useful for pre-school as well as early years (see Wechsler 2006).

The test offers subtests in the three key areas of reading:

- untimed single word accuracy
- reading comprehension
- reading speed.

Phonological Assessment Battery – Revised (PhAB-R)

PhAB-R identifies those children aged 6 years to 14 years 11 months who need help by providing an individual assessment of the child's phonological skills. It comprises six tests of phonological processing, including:

- alliteration
- naming speed
- rhyme
- spoonerisms
- fluency
- non-word reading test.

The authors claim that this test helps teachers prevent potential problems and remedy existing ones. It can also be used effectively with children who have English as an additional language (EAL). It is a useful tool and gives a good measure of how pupils are responding to interventions (see Frederickson, Frith and Reason 1997).

Phonological Assessment Battery (2nd edn: Primary) (PhAB 2)

This updated version offers a comprehensive battery of tests that help assess phonological awareness in children aged 5–11 (see Gibbs and Bodman 2014). It has four new subtests:

- Blending – combining sounds to make a spoken word.

- Phonological working memory – a child's ability to use short-term memory for phonological segments.

- Phoneme segmentation – separating spoken words into their constituent phonemes.

- Phoneme deletion – the ability to anticipate how a word would sound if one phoneme is deleted.

Helen Arkell Spelling Test Version 2 (HAST-2)

HAST-2 is a single-word spelling test developed for teachers, specialist teachers and educational psychologists to use with individuals from 5 years to adult. It can be administered individually or in groups, making it appropriate for use in schools as well as diagnostic assessments.

It contains two parallel forms as well as a longer, combined form. Standardised scores, confidence intervals, percentile ranks and age equivalents are provided. Diagnostic grids have been developed to chart error types and to assist with target setting. Support strategies for spelling are offered (see Caplan, Bark and McLean 2012).

Wide Range Achievement Test (4th edn) (WRAT-4)

The age range is from 5 upwards (see Wilkinson and Robertson 2006). WRAT-4 includes the following four subtests:

- Word reading – measures letter and word decoding through letter identification and word recognition.

- Sentence comprehension – measures an individual's ability to gain meaning from words and to comprehend ideas and information contained in sentences through the use of a modified close technique.

- Spelling – measures an individual's ability to encode sounds into written form through the use of a dictated spelling format containing both letters and words.

- Maths computation – measures an individual's ability to perform basic mathematic computations through counting, identifying numbers, solving simple oral problems and calculating written maths problems.

Wide Range Assessment of Memory and Learning (2nd edn) (WRAML2)

The age range is from 5 upwards, and this test includes subtests on picture memory recognition, design memory, verbal learning recall and recognition, story memory recall and recognition and verbal and symbolic working memory (see Sheslow and Adams 2003).

Test of Auditory Processing Skills (3rd edn) (TAPS-3)

TAPS-3 measures what a person does with 'what is heard'. It provides a way to identify particular auditory processes that the individual may be having difficulties with, allowing appropriate remediation strategies to be planned. The indices are auditory attention, basic phonological skills, auditory memory and auditory cohesion (see Martin and Brownell 2005).

Cognitive measures

One of the most well used practices in the assessment procedures for specific learning difficulties is to obtain a measure of intellectual functioning as part of the investigation into discrepancies. WISC-V is often used as an ability measure as it is well standardised and translated into a number of languages (Wechsler 2016). The WISC is a cognitive test and there is evidence that children with dyslexia can have difficulties in relation to cognition. Cognition essentially involves how children think and process information in order to understand it, to relate it to previous knowledge and to store it in long-term memory – and these factors need to be considered in an assessment.

The other factor associated with dyslexia is in the output of information. Children with dyslexia do not often perform to their full ability in tests because responding to test items involves immediate responses, many of which are in written form, and all of which have to be delivered without any help from the examiner. Yet they may respond well to cues and 'assisted assessment', which can often reveal skills and aptitudes that are concealed in traditionally administered psychometric tests.

These factors emphasise the need to used tests selectively and purposefully. While it is important to obtain measures of the extent of the difficulty, it is equally important to obtain evidence of the nature of the difficulties experienced and the reasons for these difficulties. This information is necessary if appropriate and effective intervention is to be put in place in the early years.

More specific tests can accompany some of those mentioned above and can provide diagnostic criteria as well as age/grade-related measures. One such example of this is CTOPP-2 (Wagner *et al.* 2013). Wagner *et al.* placed the test within a theoretical framework that pinpoints three types of phonological processing relevant for mastery of written language – phonological awareness, phonological memory and rapid naming.

- Phonological awareness refers to an individual's awareness of and access to the sound structure of oral language. It is often seen as one of the principal difficulties in dyslexia and some other specific learning difficulties, and studies show that children who are weak in phonological awareness display improved reading performance after being given an intervention (Torgesen, Morgan and Davis 1992; Torgesen, Wagner and Rashotte 1997).

- Phonological memory refers to coding information phonologically for temporary storage in working or short-term memory. This is often referred to as the 'phonological loop' (Baddeley 1986; Torgesen 1996). Difficulties in this area can restrict a child's abilities to learn new material. Phonological coding in working memory, according to Wagner, Torgesen and Rashotte (1999), therefore plays an important role in decoding new words, particularly multisyllabic words.

- Rapid naming relates to the efficiency with which young readers are able to retrieve phonological codes associated with individual phonemes, word segments and entire words. This is important as it has been shown that those who have difficulty in rapid naming usually have difficulty in reading fluency, and that those who have difficulty in both rapid naming and phonological awareness (double deficit) will have greater difficulty in learning to read than those with deficits in either rapid naming or phonological awareness (Bowers and Wolf 1993).

The CTOPP-2 not only provides precise diagnostic information, but can also be used as a means of monitoring and evaluating a child's progress with the intervention that is being used.

Contextualising the results

It is important to ensure that the assessment process and results from any tests used are contextualised in relation to the curriculum and the nature of the child's learning situation. Sometimes factors within the classroom and the materials that are being used may account for the difficulties the child is displaying as much as the child's own attributes. Came and Reid (2008) tackle the issue of assessing literacy from the view of identifying concern and empowering the teacher to be in a position to do this. In their publication *Concern, Assess, Provide (CAP) it All*, they provide a range of materials that can be used in the classroom context and that focus directly on the student's current work.

They ask the key question 'What is literacy?', and suggest that the answer will determine the selection of information to undertake an assessment. This can mean addressing the functional aspects of literacy (technical) or the purpose of literacy (meaning). One of the important aspects of this is to have efficient and effective monitoring mechanisms in place to ensure that all aspects of the reading process are addressed. Unlike some other tests, they include assessment of children's inferential understanding of text as well as the literal meaning of the passage. Identifying the inferences in texts is an important element for developing higher order thinking and processing skills, and is particularly important for children with dyslexia, as often their main focus tends to be on mastering the bottom-up subskills of reading, with the inferential meanings of the text sometimes lost.

This emphasises their view that assessment should not be carried out in isolation. It needs a context, a purpose and appropriate linkage with intervention. Similarly, teaching reading should not be carried out in isolation. Assessment, therefore, is the starting point, but it is important that the time allocated to assessment is used appropriately and productively. This is why it is important that a range of materials are used, and that the teacher and specialist teacher need to be empowered to take some responsibility for the assessment process – to observe, diagnose, monitor and plan an appropriate intervention based on a solid and sound framework.

The 'problem to solution' approach (Came and Reid 2008) provides a useful focus. This includes the following five areas.

Clarify the concern

- Can I define the problem?
- Who has a problem?
- Why are there concerns?
- What do I want to achieve?
- What strategies have been attempted which work/don't work?

Get your evidence

- Look at the full range of evidence already available.
- Further assess the extent of the difficulty.
- Consider further assessment.
- Establish a starting point for intervention.
- Is this a balanced view, and has everyone been consulted?

Plan for learning

- What strategies/programmes will be used?

- Who will implement them?

- What are the specific short-term targets?

- How can I involve the parents?

- Who will monitor the progress?

- How will progress be measured?

Action/implementation

- Obtain agreement from all.

- Gather the materials.

- Conduct the programme.

- Keep parents involved.

Monitor and review

- What is going well?

- When is it working?

- Has progress been measured?

- Is progress evident?

- Has monitoring informed future targets?

- Should the plan continue?

- What are the future targets?

A specific framework for assessment

The list below includes a number of areas that need to be considered in some way throughout the assessment process. The idea is that this is a comprehensive list and it needs to be adapted and contextualised for the individual requirements of the assessment, depending, of course, on the type of challenges the child displays. It is important, however, to keep an open mind when conducting an assessment and to ensure that a wide range of tests and other procedures are used, although the following can be used as a guide:

- *Sensory assessment:* Hearing, vision in particular, and especially for young children.

- *Information from parents:* This is essential as parents have much to offer and can have a very detailed understanding of their child's needs as well as their child's strengths and weaknesses. Parents need to be consulted at the outset but also throughout the assessment and particularly at the end, in the feedback session.

- *Word recognition test:* This is important as it can be a good test of decoding skills. The child is not able to use context as only individual words are presented. The child has to either decode the word, read it visually, or access the word from his or her established lexicon. This type of basic reading test can also be a useful diagnostic instrument, and an attempt should always be made to analyse the type of reading errors made.

- *Non-word recognition test:* This is a pure test of decoding. Because non-words are used, learners will not be able to read them visually or have seen them before so they have to decode them. This will provide an indication of their phonological skills and their understanding of word rules.

- *Spelling test:* It is always important to use a spelling test – perhaps several – as spelling errors can be diagnostic and can reveal a great deal about the learner's literacy development. Try to identify a pattern of errors, for example, the use of silent letters, word endings, plurals, vowel digraphs and spelling rules. WIAT-II has a good word spelling test, and the Test of Orthographic Competence (TOC) (Mather *et al.* 2008) focuses on visual spelling ability by providing part of the word and the child has to complete the word – this is essentially a visual spelling test. It is also important to use a spelling in context test so you can compare the child's spelling using single words with his or her spelling in a piece of free writing.

- *Phonological assessment:* This is particularly important for younger children and very important if dyslexia is suspected. There are a great number of appropriate phonological tests but they should show if the child recognises beginning, mid and end sounds in words, and if they can recognise the onset and rime parts of words. Rhyming is important in a phonological test and you should be able to obtain information that can reveal whether the child is able to recognise and generate rhymes.

- *Miscue analysis:* The assessment should be diagnostic as well as standardised; miscue analysis, irrespective of the particular system or code used, is a very useful tool that can be used to analyse reading errors and obtain a pattern of difficulties.

- *Reading/listening comprehension test:* Both reading and listening comprehension are important. In some cases, as might be found in children who have severe dyslexia, listening comprehension can be the most useful as it does not include being able to read accurately. However, it is interesting than many children who may not score high in terms of reading accuracy can perform quite well in reading comprehension, and their score is often higher than their accuracy score. It is important that both are used.

- *Free writing:* This can be very revealing and informative. There are many different things to look for here, for example, writing speed, spelling errors, grammar and punctuation, quality of writing in terms of content, the use of vocabulary and the structure of the written work. WIAT-II has a number of writing tasks for all ages of children and young adults. The ones for the younger children are highly structured and may involve joining sentences together as well as sentence generation. For older children titles are provided and they have to write a story based on these titles.

- *Curriculum information:* It is important to contextualise the assessment and to include information obtained from the child's performance in class. Communication with the class teacher is therefore crucial.

- *Observational assessment:* This is important for identifying at risk children in literacy, numeracy, movement and attention factors, as these can all be incorporated into an observational schedule that can be implemented in the assessment.

- *Movement assessment:* This is particularly important if information on both fine and gross motor skills is required. Fine motor skills involve handwriting and delicate tasks such as the bead threading task in the Dyslexia Screening Test (DST), and this type of task can have relevance for dyslexia. Gross motor skills involve body awareness and spatial awareness and can often be noted in extreme clumsiness and coordination difficulties.

- *Number assessment:* It is important to carry out several different types of number assessments, which include mental number work and also problem-solving skills using both concrete practical tools and materials.

- *Attention issues:* Information on 'attention' can also be noted through observation and through testing. The digit span subtest can also be a test of attention, as can any of the speed tests used, but test observation is also very important.

- *Environment factors:* It has already been indicated that it is important at this early stage to look at the learning environment as well as within-child factors. Aspects of the environment that need to be considered include the layout of the rooms; learning opportunities as well as opportunities to explore learning; social groupings and opportunities for peer interaction; and the ambience within the room, such as music, colour, light, pictures and space.

It is important to go into an assessment with a fairly open mind and to see it as a problem-solving exercise. While it is useful to have an established test battery, it is useful if you can see that battery as flexible and not fixed. You may not need to use the full battery for every assessment, and there are some assessments when, for whatever reason, you may have to use a test you may not normally use. It is important to seek information from as many sources as possible and use as many relevant tests as possible.

Formative/informal assessment

Formative assessment can be complementary to the use of more formal tests. It is usually informal, although not always, but there is scope for the use of more informal measures in this type of formative assessment. Informal assessments can provide teachers with opportunities to:

- notice what is happening during learning activities

- recognise how the child is progressing with learning

- work out how they can help to take that learning further and develop their skills.

This provides the opportunity for teachers to become 'reflective practitioners'. It is generally accepted that reflective practitioners can notice what is different or unusual about patterns of progress in student learning. They think carefully and deeply about what assessment information is telling them about the child's understanding, and also more particularly about their own teaching and what they should or can do differently to connect to and respond to the thinking of each child.

The assessment process and results from any tests used should be contextualised in relation to the curriculum and the nature of the child's learning situation.

Strategies and materials for the formal assessment of dyslexia

Phonological assessment

This can largely be carried out by the teacher from teacher-adapted materials or, indeed, through observation of the child's reading pattern. It covers the following areas:

- non-word reading

- sound recognition

- syllable segmentation

- recognising prefixes, suffixes and syllables

- rhyme recognition and production

- phoneme segmentation such as blending, and recognition of initial and final phonemes.

Screening/baseline assessment

There are some issues that can be raised in relation to screening and baseline assessment. These include:

- What is the most desirable age (or ages) for children to be screened?

- Which skills, abilities and attainments in performance should children be screened for?

- How should the results of any screening procedures be used?

It is important that the results of screening and baseline assessments are used diagnostically and not to prematurely label children. There are some screening tests that have been developed specifically to identify the possibility of dyslexia. These can yield very useful information but should be used in conjunction with other data obtained from observations made by the teacher of the child's work as well as progress in class and in different areas of the curriculum.

Informal checklists

This form of assessment can provide some general data on the broad areas of difficulty experienced by the child. For example, the teacher may decide the child has a pronounced difficulty in the use of contextual cues, but this does not provide information as to why this difficulty persists and the kind of difficulties the pupil experiences. Does the child use contextual cues on some occasions, and under certain conditions? The teacher would be required to carry out further investigations to obtain some further explanations of the difficulty.

Information processing

Children with dyslexia often experience difficulty with what is known as information processing, the interaction between the learner and the task. The information processing cycle has three main components:

- *Input:* How the information is received – auditory, visual, tactile and kinaesthetic.

- *Cognition:* Memory, understanding, organising and making sense of information.

- *Output:* Talking, reading aloud, discussing, drawing, observing and experiencing.

Children with dyslexia can have difficulties at all three stages of this cycle. It is important, therefore, to draw on diagnostic and observational data that involve these three stages. It can be useful to acknowledge this when identifying the difficulties experienced by the child. For example, one can ask whether the same difficulties are experienced if the material is presented visually as opposed to auditory. Perhaps the young child can learn more effectively if he or she is able to experience the actual learning through the kinaesthetic modality – most young children are kinaesthetic, that is, they need to experience the activity. Although this is related to teaching approaches, it is crucial that this is acknowledged in the identification and assessment process as it is important that reasons for the difficulty are sought, and that a clear link can be forged between assessment and teaching approaches.

Suggestions for linking assessment with intervention
Input

- Identify the student's preferred learning style, particularly visual, auditory, kinaesthetic or tactile preferences, as these can be crucial in how information is presented. It is important to present new information in the learner's preferred modality.

- Present new information in small steps – this will ensure that the short-term memory does not become overloaded with information before it is fully consolidated.

- New material will need to be repeatedly presented through over-learning (i.e., repetition until mastery is reached). This does not mean that the repetition should be in the same form; rather, it is important that it should be varied using as wide a range of materials and strategies as possible.

- It is a good idea to present the key points at the initial stage of learning new material. This helps to provide a framework for the new material and can help to relate new information to previous knowledge.

Cognition

- Information should be related to previous knowledge. This ensures that concepts are developed and the learner can place the information into a learning framework or schema. Successful learning is often due to efficient organisation of information. It is important, therefore, to group information together and to show the connection between the two. For example, if the topic to be covered was the Harry Potter series of books, then concepts such as witchcraft and magic, and the words associated with these, would need to be explained and some of the related ideas discussed. This should be done prior to reading the text.

- Some specific memory strategies, such as mind mapping and mnemonics, can be used to help the learner remember some of the key words or more challenging ideas.

Output

- Often children with specific learning difficulties have difficulty identifying the key points in new learning or in a text. This can be overcome by providing the child with these key points or words at the beginning stage of learning the new material. Additionally the learner can acquire skills in this by practising using summaries. Each period of new learning should be summarised by the learner – this in itself helps to identify the key points.

- It may also be beneficial to measure progress orally rather than in writing, particularly with in-class continuous assessment. It is not unusual for children with dyslexia to be much more proficient orally than in written form. Oral presentation of information can therefore help to instil confidence. By contrast, a written exercise can often be damaging in terms of confidence, unless considerable preparation and planning have helped ensure that some of the points indicated above are put into place.

Examples of checklists

Pre-school stage

Houston (2004) has provided extremely useful guidelines based on practice used by Edinburgh City Council in Scotland. Among the other strategies she recommends, she provides a checklist, and some of the main components are shown below:

- Poor language and pronunciation
- Poor rhyming
- Immature speech pattern and communication
- Poor phonological awareness
- Poor concept of time
- Poor organisation
- Poor listening skills
- Poor memory for rhymes, stories, events and instructions
- Cannot clap a rhythm or keep a musical beat
- Is clumsy, wriggly and accident prone
- Is hard to engage, and shows little interest in activities
- Can be easily distracted
- Has poor posture
- Poor fine motor skills, including drawing, copying and letter formation
- Poor eye tracking and inability to converge from far to near
- Poor spatial concepts
- Poor body image
- Has not established hand dominance
- Has poor ball skills
- Has poor balance and coordination

- Poor letter knowledge
- Social skills are very limited or unsuccessful

Lower primary stage (ages 5–8)

- Finds it hard to learn letter/sound relationships
- Confuses letters or words with similar shapes or sounds
- Finds it hard to sound out simple words
- Reverses, inserts or omits words, letters and numbers
- Has difficulty with spelling very simple regular words
- Muddles the order of letters and words
- Keeps losing the place when reading
- Reads and does written work very slowly
- Has difficulty pronouncing longer common words
- Has difficulty hearing rhymes and sounds within words
- Has poorly spaced, poorly formed, large font or small heavily indented writing
- Has difficulty memorising (especially in number work) despite adequate supported in-school practice
- Is slow to learn to tell the time
- Is slow to learn to tie shoe laces
- Confuses left/right and up/down
- Has difficulty learning the alphabet, months and days in order
- Has delayed or idiosyncratic speech and language development
- Has difficulty carrying out an oral instruction or, more commonly, multiple oral instructions
- Has poor organising ability – losing and forgetting things

- Has poor coordination and depth perception – tripping and bumping into things

- Has word-finding difficulties

- Has behaviour difficulties, frustration and poor self-image

- Is easily distracted – either hyperactive or daydreaming

- Other – please give details

Concluding thoughts

- There are a number of different stages to an assessment, such as observation, screening, standardised assessment (attainments and cognitive) and informal assessment (such as curriculum-focused).

- It is important to look at the barriers to learning experienced by the child.

- Early identification is crucial as it can lead to early intervention, and it is useful to note the 'at risk' factors for dyslexia.

- The Assess, Plan, Do, Review procedure is useful.

- Consider the classroom environment and the impact of the environment on the learner.

- Try to link assessment with intervention as much as possible.

Chapter 4

Intervention Approaches
Meeting Individual Needs

The early years focus on individual needs

This chapter looks at specific and specialised approaches for literacy and learning that can be accessed to support children with dyslexia. Chapter 5 then emphasises the role of the curriculum, learning strategies and the learning environment. Although they are in separate chapters the two factors, the child and the learning environment, interact and should not be seen in isolation.

The *Independent Review of the Teaching of Early Reading* (Rose 2006) strongly advocated high-quality, systematic phonic work that should be taught individually. Phonic work, the report suggested, should be set within a broad language-rich curriculum that takes full account of developing the four interdependent strands of language – speaking, listening, reading and writing – and therefore enlarging children's stock of words. These factors can be implemented for all in the nursery/ early years setting, as all children will benefit from these. Ideally, for a programme or an approach to be of maximum benefit to teachers, it should be easily understood and implemented, but also flexible and adaptable to different contexts and types of dyslexic difficulties.

The Rose Review: Identifying and Teaching Children and Young People with Dyslexia and Literacy Difficulties (Rose 2009) defined dyslexia as a learning difficulty that primarily affects the skills involved in accurate and fluent word reading and spelling. The report indicated that the characteristic features of dyslexia are difficulties in phonological awareness, verbal memory and verbal processing speed. It has already been shown in the previous chapter how these factors can be identified.

The Rose Review came down heavily on the side of synthetic phonics, and there is an abundance of materials that can assist with this. Using this method, children are taught to read letters or groups of letters by saying the sound(s) they represent. They can then start to read words by blending (synthesising) the sounds together to make a word.

One popular programme is Jolly Phonics (Lloyd and Wernham 1998), which has been regularly updated and new materials developed. It was originally developed for children from pre-school to age 7. Basically it involves sound recognition, auditory training and writing – children listen to the sounds in words and then write the letters that relate to these sounds. Jolly Phonics is now used in many countries, including the US.

Other publications include *Jolly Songs (Jolly Phonics)*,[1] *Jolly Stories*,[2] *Jolly Phonics Workbooks*,[3] *My First Letter Sounds*[4] and *Jolly Phonics Activity Books*. *Jolly Phonics Parent/Teacher Guide* (Jolly Learning no date) provides advice on using the programme for both parents and teachers. It focuses on five basic skills in reading: learning the letter sounds, learning letter formation, blending, identifying sounds in words, and spelling tricky words. Although these skills are separate, they are taught together. The idea behind Jolly Phonics is that the 42 main sounds in English are taught and not just the alphabet. Each sound has an action that helps the child remember the letters it represents. Eventually the child will no longer need the actions.

There is a great deal of additional material such as Blending Cards and the *Jolly Phonics Word Book*.[5] These materials are ideal because they involve the whole class and the child who is having difficulty acquiring literacy will still be able to participate in some way using these materials. Progression can be monitored using the *Jolly Readers*.[6]

While *Jolly Phonics* is an excellent set of materials and can be used by all at the beginning stage of literacy, the materials from the Nessy camp are more focused on dyslexia and are used internationally. Nessy has been making educational software for children for many years now and is the winner of a number of educational awards. Nessy uses strategies

1   See www.amazon.co.uk/Jolly-Songs-Phonics/dp/1844140695
2   See http://jollylearning.co.uk/jolly-shop/jolly-stories
3   See http://jollylearning.co.uk/jolly-shop/jolly-phonics-workbook-1
4   See http://jollylearning.co.uk/jolly-shop/my-first-letter-sounds
5   See http://jollylearning.co.uk/jolly-shop/jolly-phonics-word-book
6   See http://jollylearning.co.uk/jolly-shop/jolly-readers-level-1-complete-se

and games and all the programmes are developed in the classroom; the approach has been successful in motivating reluctant readers. Nessy has also proven to be successful for bilingual learners.

In Canada and the US the Orton-Gillingham approach to teaching has been prevalent. It has grown from the work of Dr Samuel Orton, an American neuropsychiatrist and neuropathologist (1879–1948), who was a pioneer in investigating dyslexia (see Henry and Brickley 1999). Dr Orton understood dyslexia as a neurological condition that required treatment through education. In the late 1920s he worked with Anna Gillingham, an educational psychologist, to formulate an approach to teaching students with dyslexia based on multisensory, structured, prescriptive teaching of the elements of language. These principles of instruction guided successful intervention with students and the formation of the Orton-Gillingham (or OG) approach to teaching, now generalised as Multisensory Structured Language, or MSL.

According to Corey Zylstra from the REACH Learning Centre in Western Canada, who is herself an international trainer in OG and has helped to develop an Arabic version, the OG/MSL approach is now widely used in a number of countries around the world, not only as a necessary intervention approach for those with dyslexia, but also as a scientifically sound, evidence-based approach to teaching reading and spelling to all students. Zylstra indicates that the OG/MSL approach can be particularly beneficial for kindergarten children because educators focus on *how* to teach using a multisensory, structured, sequential approach to ensure that children have opportunities to discover important elements of the language (personal communication). This is followed by ample guided support to reinforce new information – using multisensory techniques.

OG/MSL educators also focus on *what* to teach, ensuring that all children are provided with direct instruction in phonological and phonemic awareness, phonics, fluency, vocabulary and comprehension. Corey Zylstra made the point that research shows (e.g., Joshi, Dahlgren and Boulware-Gooden 2002) that solid instruction in phonological and phonemic awareness followed by phonics using the OG/MSL approach in early years of pre-school through 1st grade can reduce the later impact of struggles with literacy. This kind of evidence-based instruction not only helps with the early identification of children who may be at risk for dyslexia, but also benefits all early learners by providing them with the necessary framework for later success with reading. On the OG approach, one teacher attending a workshop on understanding the language of the programme and how to teach it, as opposed to just facilitating it, indicated that 'it is an invaluable tool to bettering our teaching and [developing] literacy development in our students. If every teacher had this knowledge there would be more mastery at a younger age and less of those we find in grades 4 and 5 who continue to struggle with the basics'.[7]

This also underlines the important point that the rationale and the concepts underlining a programme need to be understood before effective implementation can be carried out.

Miller Guron and Lundberg (2004) indicated that those learners who have been exposed to phonological awareness instruction prior to the age of three are likely to develop more effective processing of both languages than those who have learned later. It appears that explicit multisensory teaching is the most successful (Mahfoudhi and Haynes 2009), with evidence that training in phoneme and letter knowledge for at risk learners can help them to catch up with normally developing readers (Caravolas et al. 2012).

Stages of reading development

In order to identify the nature of the child's challenges in literacy it is useful to look specifically at the different stages of reading development. This will help to pinpoint the particular areas within the reading process the child is struggling with. Frith (1985, 2002) identifies the following developmental stages in the acquisition of reading skills.

Logographic stage

The child makes use of visual recognition of overall word patterns – this means that he or she is able to recognise words as units. This may not necessarily mean that the child can reproduce these words accurately (this would be an alphabetic skill), and as a result the child can easily misspell words he or she is able to read.

---

7   Extracted from REACH website https://www.reachlearningcentre.com/from-workshops.

Alphabetic stage

The child tackles the sound/symbol correspondence. Ehri (1999) suggests that the alphabetic stage can be divided into four phases that capture the changes that occur in the development of sight word reading: pre-alphabetic, partial alphabetic, full alphabetic and consolidated alphabetic. Each phase is labelled to reflect the predominant type of connection that links the written forms of sight words to their pronunciations and meanings in memory. Therefore, during the pre-alphabetic phase, beginning readers remember how to read sight words by forming connections between selected visual attributes of words and their pronunciations or meanings. Letter–sound relations are not involved in the connections. When pre-alphabetic readers read print in their environment, such as stop signs and fast food restaurant signs, they do this, according to Ehri, by remembering visual cues accompanying the print rather than the written words themselves.

The next phase is the partial alphabetic phase. Here beginning readers remember how to read sight words by forming partial alphabetic connections between only some of the letters in written words and sounds detected in their pronunciations. Because first and final letters are especially salient, these are often the cues that are remembered. To remember sight words in this way, partial alphabetic readers need to know some letter–sound correspondences and have some phonemic segmentation.

During the next phase, the full alphabetic phase, beginners remember how to read sight words by forming complete grapho-phonemic connections. This is possible because readers know how the major graphemes symbolise phonemes in the conventional spelling system (Venezky 1999). In applying this knowledge to form connections for sight words, spellings become fully bonded to pronunciations in memory. The final phase, according to Ehri, is the full alphabetic phase when readers are able to decode words by transforming graphemes into phonemes, and they are able to retain sight words in memory by connecting graphemes to phonemes. The consolidated alphabetic stage acquaints them with the pronunciations of syllabic and sub-syllabic spelling patterns that recur in different words. The letters in these patterns become consolidated into larger spelling–sound units that can be used to decode words and to retain sight words in memory.

Orthographic stage

The orthographic stage refers to the spelling patterns of words. The child possesses and comprehends knowledge of the letter–sound relationship as well as structure and meaning. This means that as well as being aware of rules, the child can also use cues and context.

It has been argued that children with dyslexia can find the alphabetic stage difficult because the sound–symbol correspondence rests to a great extent on skills in phonics. So before children acquire a competent understanding of the relationship between letter units (graphemes) and sound units (phonemes), they need a degree of phonological awareness (Snowling 2000).

Frith (2002) puts forward the view that writing and the desire to write helps to enhance the alphabetic stage of reading because spelling is linked more directly to the alphabetic principle and letter–sound relationships.

The alphabetic reader, according to Snowling (2000), may also find difficulty reading words that have inconsistent orthographic patterns, but that are pronounced in the same way. Similarly, irregular words are mispronounced (e.g., 'island' would be pronounced 'is-land'). This developmental aspect of reading serves to illustrate the importance of the procedure of error analysis and identifying the type and pattern of errors made by children with difficulties in reading.

Some key educational needs

Some key needs are usually the areas where the child with 'high risk' of dyslexia would have some difficulties:

- Letter recognition.

    » Segmentation – breaking the word down into its constituent sounds.

    » Blending – joining the letters together to make a word, for example B_U_S together make bus.

    » Phonemic awareness – awareness of the sounds in words and eventually being aware of where these sounds come in the words.

    » Grapheme-phoneme correspondence – this relates the visual image to the sound of the word.

- Word recognition.

  » Recognition of word patterns – this can be simple regular patterns or more irregular patterns and patterns that require knowledge of spelling rules.

  » Use of visual memory skills – some words can only be read visually, for example, the word 'guess' will cause problems phonetically and is one that is commonly spelt phonetically by young children as 'gess'.

Mahfoudhi and Haynes (2009), quoting the National Reading Panel (2000) in the US, argue that explicit structured phonics instruction – teaching of rules that link speech information with letters and letter patterns – improves word recognition skills and contributes to spelling, decoding fluency and reading comprehension in typically developing children as well as children with dyslexia and related language learning difficulties.

Visual factors

Holland (2010) and Holland and Holland (2016) provide a strong case for the visual component in dyslexia. Often coloured overlays are used almost automatically if a child is suspected of dyslexia. They argue, however, that there is much more to visual difficulties in relation to dyslexia than, for example, the use of coloured overlays, that it is important to understand the visual system and the role of the magnocellular (peripheral and background awareness) and pavlocellular (awareness of details and specific items) pathways to understand the nature of the child's difficulties in accessing print fluently. They estimate that between 10 and 15 per cent of the child population have visual inefficiencies that impact on learning, and suggest that some indicators, such as the following, may be helpful:

- Often loses the place when reading.

- Misses out words or re-reads the same word.

- Needs to use a finger or marker to keep their place.

- Quickly becomes tired when reading.

- Experiences transient blurred or double vision during close work.

- Complains of words 'moving about', 'shimmering' or 'dancing' when reading.

- Has difficulty copying from the board down on to paper.

- Complains of a headache (usually around the temples) after close work.

- Has poor concentration for close work.

- Has a short and often decreasing working distance.

- Continuous reading is inaccurate, yet can read single words quite easily.

- Has difficulty 'taking in' what is being read, and has to read something several times for meaning.

Approaches and activities

Phonological processing

Activities for phonological awareness include rhyming activities, blending and segmenting of words into onset and rime, games involving blending, segmenting and deleting phonemes as well as exercises to help with the recognition of alliteration, sound patterns and rhyme within words. Children practise identifying initial and final sounds in words, and eventually practise blending longer words.

For phonic skills, the THRASS (Teaching Handwriting, Reading and Spelling Skills) programme can be useful.[8] It has some excellent activities for parents.

Very popular game activities that focus on synthetic phonics to support literacy are called Trugs (Teach Reading Using Games),[9] which can be used by teachers (Trugs at Schools) and parents (Trugs at Home). These are structured, decodable card games that combine the professional phonics side of learning to decode print with the fun side of playing card games in a hugely effective and engaging way.

---

8   See www.thrass.co.uk
9   See www.readsuccessfully.com/what-is-trugs

Pupils are able to practise reading by sounding out the phonemes in a word from left to right and blending them together all through the word until they can read the word automatically. Trugs give them an enjoyable and successful way to reinforce and consolidate the knowledge of their letter–sound correspondences. There are three boxes in Trugs and Box 1 is appropriate for beginning readers and early years. It introduces letter sounds and eventually two-syllable words. Trugs games focus on synthetic phonics following the government's guidelines for teaching early reading skills (Rose 2006). They have reached the international market and are used in many countries including Europe, Australia and Asia.

The Brain Box® range of games is excellent for young children who may have dyslexia.[10] What is extremely useful is that they do not need any real skills in literacy – the games are very visual and rely on problem-solving skills; indeed, the child with literacy difficulties or dyslexia may actually excel at this type of activity. This means that in addition to helping with language and literacy, the games can help with self-esteem and motivation. There is a good range of games for ages 3–6, such as the Brain Box Alphabet Jigsaw, and there are also activities for ages 7 and up.

Onset/rime

This involves the prefix and the rest of the word and dividing words into syllables. This is helpful in developing and extending decoding skills and for transferring rules and new word endings learned to other words in the same word family. The Oxford Reading Tree[11] is useful for this.

Sight word and paired reading

This involves breaking down words into constituent sounds in order to read them. This requires a great deal of exposure to whole words, and approaches such as paired reading can be very useful. Using paired reading the child can hear the word and see it and say it all at the same time. One of the key principles of paired reading is that it is

---

10   See www.brainbox.co.uk/brainbox-range/age-3-6
11   See https://global.oup.com/education/content/primary/series/oxford-reading-tree/?region=uk

multisensory – the text can be seen, heard and articulated at the same time. Additionally, since the adult is usually taking the lead, they will also apply expression and meaning to the text and this can enhance comprehension.

The procedures for paired reading are shown below, and can be easily carried out by parents, teaching assistants and teachers.

Studies indicate an increase in reading accuracy, fluency and expression through the use of paired reading. In addition, research indicates that children find the method easy to use, and feel they are more competent readers as a result. The procedure is as follows:

At the first reading session:

- Student and tutor agree on reading times.
- They also agree on a starting signal.
- Tutor reviews how the technique works.

Before reading:

- Student chooses reading materials and can change them at any time.
- The find a quiet spot away from distractions.

Paired reading:

- Always begin by reading together.
- Non-critical correction of errors works best: if an error is made, the tutor says the word and the student repeats it.

Reading solo:

- Student and tutor agree on a solo reading signal.
- Tutor praises the student when the signal is used.
- Tutor continues to offer support and praise during solo reading.

Return to paired reading:

- Tutor corrects student's mistake (gives word and student repeats it).
- Return to paired reading until the student signals to go solo again.

'Talk':

- Student should remember to relax and talk about what she or he has read.

Listening and comprehension skills

It is important that children who are struggling with reading obtain as much practice as possible in listening and responding to text and questions. Discussion is the key here and the child may not be able to read, but the language experience element is crucial, and comprehension can follow on from this. This is particularly important for children who may be deprived of reading on their own because of difficulties in accessing print.

Spelling and writing skills

While it is not expected that pre-school children should be competent in spelling, they should be making a start in joining and sequencing some letters together. This builds up word families and then they are off! For example, the letters AT can be taught and this can lead to being able to spell MAT, CAT, etc. Children with dyslexia will experience difficulties with this and will perform inconsistently – sometimes getting it correct and at other times wrong. A large range of two-syllable words can be built up before children start school so the difference between those children and children at risk of dyslexia can be readily noted.

Pencil control can be a good indicator of children at high risk of dyslexia. I recall a presentation by Evans (1989) (at that time a special needs education adviser in Glamorgan) at the first BDA International Conference. He firmly stated that he found the task of colouring in a clown at pre-school level a good discriminator between those who were advancing well and those who were at risk of dyslexia. While more sophisticated tasks can be used and the screening tests discussed in Chapter 3, this type of task still has many uses. It can, for example, identify if the child has motor control or not. Certainly at ages 4–5 children should be printing letters, and even at around 3 they should be able to trace letters.

Two aspects can develop early writing skills – the actual practice of drawing (lines, circles, squares, etc.) and developing fine motor control through exercises and developing muscle control and hand/eye coordination. Joining dots or games involving mazes can be useful for developing pencil control, and screwing lids on jars and other types of similar tasks can help with fine motor control, as can playing with Play-Doh.

Computer programs

Computer programs can be very user friendly and introduce a fun element to learning. There is an increasing amount of excellent computer programs that can help with reading, writing, spelling and maths. Computer programs can also provide learners with a degree of independence and practice at working on their own. Programs such as Kidspiration™ can be useful for children at risk of dyslexia.[12] Kidspiration encourages exploration and understanding of words, mind mapping, numbers and concepts, and text help can provide support for spelling, planning and developing written work.

A good review of software can be found on SuperKids®.[13] There are quite a number of programs for early years, with many focusing on phonics.

Methods of teaching reading

The most popular methods to teach reading include:

- phonic or phonically based

- Look and Say – reading through sight word recognition

- language experience – using context, background knowledge and language understanding.

Phonic or phonically based

The phonic method highlights the importance of phonology and the sounds of letters and letter combinations. Jolly Phonics has produced

---

12   See www.inspiration.com/Kidspiration
13   See www.superkids.com/aweb/pages/reviews/reading

a *Pupil/Student Checklist* for this,[14] and this can be used to note the progress of each child. Phonic methods can help children who have an obvious difficulty in mastering and remembering sound blends and vowel digraphs and who have difficulty in synthesising them to make a word. Children with dyslexia will likely experience difficulties in merging the two components of reading (i.e., knowledge of sound and knowledge of language) to facilitate a meaningful reading experience.

Chall and Popp (1996) emphasise the need to teach phonics, and argue that if taught well it is highly meaningful – through phonics children can get close to the sound of a word and through that to the meaning of the word. They suggest a systematic phonics approach from pre-school, with related activities set within a total reading programme. This is consistent with *The Rose Review* (2009) that also recommended synthetic phonics.

Frith (1995) emphasises the nature of the phonological 'core variable' in literacy learning and particularly how it is associated with dyslexia. The causal model framework (Frith 2002) highlights the distinctiveness of phonological competence by focusing on three levels for assessing phonological difficulties: biological observations about brain functioning, at the cognitional level in relation to the hypothetical constructs of intellectual ability and phonological processing ability, and at the behavioural level in relation to performance in assessments such as phonological awareness tests, naming speed tests, and non-word, reading and spelling tests.

Support for the phonological core variable model as an explanation of the difficulties associated with dyslexia has led to illuminative research activity and the development of phonological skills training programmes (Henry 2003; Reason and Frederickson 1996; Sawyer and Bernstein 2008).

Look and Say

Look and Say methods emphasise exposure to print on the grounds that children will become familiar with words and build up a sight vocabulary with increased exposure. The emphasis is therefore on meaningful units of language rather than sounds of speech.

---

14   See http://jollylearning.co.uk/gallery/jolly-phonics-pupil-student-checklist

This type of method therefore requires attractive books that can become progressively more demanding. Flashcards and pictures can be used in the initial stages. The method, however, assumes a good memory for shapes of letters and words as well as the ability to master many of the irregularities of spelling and sound–symbol correspondence, which may be difficult for children with dyslexic difficulties, particularly since their memory may be weak and can rapidly become overloaded. Some elements of the phonic approaches can accompany most Look and Say methods.

Language experience

Language experience methods focus on the use of language, both oral and written, as an aid to learning to read through various modes of language enrichment. This helps the reader develop important language concepts and schemata, which in turn help to bring meaning to print. Although the child may have a decoding problem, the experience gained in language can help to compensate for this and bring some meaning to the text. This model engages the child in the process of going from thought to speech and then to encoding in print and from print to reading. Ehri (1999), however, suggests that there are three essential interrelated ingredients in the knowledge base for teachers that help to inform them in making decisions on reading instruction. These are:

- knowledge about the reading process

- knowledge about teaching methods and how these facilitate the reading process

- knowledge about observational procedures to identify the processes that readers are facilitating and the processes they have difficulty with.

Knowledge of the reading process is important, but it is equally important to relate this knowledge to classroom practices and particularly to observing how children relate to the reading process in the class.

What works for children and young people with literacy difficulties

Brooks' report *What Works for Children and Young People with Literacy Difficulties?* (2013) looks at the effectiveness of intervention schemes, focusing on both mainstream and specialist individualised programmes. In the evaluation 74 studies were analysed and each is detailed in the report. Brooks looks at 26 schemes at primary level – Year 1 and 2 schemes for reading and writing, including the following:

A.R.R.O.W.™

Children work individually on laptops and hear the text, then say and record it and play it back. They also write down the piece of text. This is more successful further up the school, but the results are impressive.[15]

AcceleRead/AcceleWrite app

This was originally developed from a 'talking computer' project from the Education Authority in Jersey, with the target group those children with dyslexic-like difficulties. It involves fun activities with cards with different phonic sounds. The letters are typed onto the computer and audio feedback is given to the child. This is probably more successful from Year 2 onwards, but the data from the use of this program have been impressive.[16]

Better Reading Partnerships

Better Reading Partnerships is a one-to-one programme that looks at phonics and phonological awareness, reading behaviours when reading text and writing skills, and can be used by Year 1 pupils. It is good for home–school partnerships and has a range of resources to promote home reading.[17]

---

15   See www.arrowtuition.co.uk

16   See www.iansyst.co.uk/technology/iansyst%27s-product-innovations/acceleread-accelewrite

17   See http://learning.gov.wales/docs/learningwales/publications/121108better readingen.pdf

Catch Up® Literacy

This is a literacy intervention programme for struggling readers from the age of 6. It is a one-on-one, 15-minute individual programme administered twice weekly, either by a teaching assistant or teacher. It has been very successful and also contains an assessment procedure.[18]

Cued Spelling

Cued Spelling[19] was originally developed by Keith Topping and colleagues at the University of Dundee (Topping 2001a).[20] This involves a pair who might be a parent and child, teacher and child or two children working together. Topping suggests that 7-year-old children can be trained to do this in half an hour (Brooks 2013, p.31).

The steps for Cued Spelling are as follows:

1. Pupils select a word to learn or are given target words.

2. Pairs enter the words into their spelling diaries.

3. Pairs read the word together.

4. Speller and helper choose cues together.

5. Pairs repeat cues aloud

6. Speller says cues while helper writes word.

7. Helper says cues while speller writes word.

8. Speller writes word quickly and says cues aloud.

9. Speller writes word quickly.

10. Speller reads word aloud.

The technique also includes daily reviews where the pupil writes all the words for the day and checks them. The wrong words are then noted and the pupil goes through the ten steps again for these words. The Cued Spelling technique is highly interactive and attempts to eliminate the fear of failure through the use of prompt correction procedures.

---

18   See www.catchup.org/interventions/literacy.php

19   See www.interventionsforliteracy.org.uk/home/interventions/list-view/cued-spelling

20   See www.dundee.ac.uk/esw/research/resources/thinkingreadingwriting

Lexia

This is a popular and established personalised learning computer program that is used successfully in many countries.[21] A research project in Cumbria, for example, showed great gains in reading accuracy among the children involved (see Brooks 2013).

Paired Reading

This is a simple yet very successful intervention. Brooks cites Topping's well-known Kirklees Project as evidence of its success. It is a popular method as the child can see the word, hear it and say it simultaneously. It is also very interactive and this is also beneficial for young children.[22]

Phono-Graphix®

The program developed by Diane McGuiness in 1997 teaches the phonological skills of blending, segmenting and phoneme manipulation, and teaches sound to symbol correspondence explicitly.[23] Brooks reports on useful progress using this in Year 1 for reading accuracy.

Read Write Inc.

This is a synthetic phonics program focusing on reading, writing and spelling. It is structured, intensive and systematic and some promising results have appeared.[24]

Reading Intervention Programme

This is one of the earlier projects on reading assessment and intervention based on Sound Linkage (Hatcher 2001). Sound Linkage

---

21 See www.lexialearning.com/solutions/literacy-improvement-pre-k-5 and also www.lexiauk.co.uk

22 For a colourful quick guide to Paired Reading, see www.educationscotland.gov.uk/Images/ScotlandReadsParentsLeaflet_tcm4-506434.pdf

23 See www.phono-graphix.com

24 See www.ruthmiskin.com/en

is a combination of phonological training and reading practice. Lessons include story work linking sounds with words.[25]

Reading Recovery

Reading Recovery[26] is an early reading and writing intervention programme, developed by Marie Clay, which focuses on children who, after one year at school, have lagged significantly behind their peers in reading and writing. Clay originally introduced the programme in New Zealand and it has since been used in many other countries. It aims to boost the reading attainment of selected children over a relatively short period, around 12 to 20 weeks, with specially trained teachers carrying out the programme, seeing children on an individual basis for 30 minutes daily. The programme centres round the individual child's strengths and weaknesses as assessed by the actual reading programme. It utilises both bottom-up and top-down reading approaches and therefore encourages the use of decoding strategies through the use of phonics, and awareness of meaning through an awareness of the context and language of the text.

It is also important that the child is helped to develop a self-improving system. This would encourage the child to:

- be aware of his or her own learning

- take control and responsibility for his or her own learning.

The goal of teaching reading is to assist the child to produce effective strategies for working on text, and according to Clay, this can be done through focusing on the practices of self-correcting and self-monitoring. The main components of the programme include:

- learning about direction

- locating and focusing on aspects of print

- spatial layout of books

- writing stories

- learning sounds in words

- comprehension and cut-up stories

---

25   See www.thereadinginterventionprogramme.org.uk

26   See www.ucl.ac.uk/international-literacy/reading-recovery

- reading books

- using print as a cue

- sound and letter sequence

- word analysis

- fluency.

A typical Reading Recovery lesson would include the analysis of the child's decoding strategies, the encouragement of fluent reading through the provision of opportunities to link sounds and letters, the reading of familiar texts and the introduction of new books.

Below is an extract I received from a teacher of a child I was working with. The name has been changed for confidentiality reasons, but it can be noted that the initial findings seem to be quite promising.

APRIL 17TH

Andrew started in Reading Recovery lessons on Monday. Reading Recovery is an early literacy intervention that helps Grade One and Two students get off to a good start in reading and writing. The Observation Survey of Early Literacy Achievement[27] is an assessment tool that focuses on children's emerging literacy and allows us to see their strengths in reading and writing.

At the end of the month Andrew knew most of the upper and lower case letters by name. He had a few confusions: p for q, n for u and b for d. It was interesting to note that he had two other confusions but was able to self-correct those.

They were: O for Q (self-corrected) and v for y (self-corrected). For the letter 'w' he gave the word 'wave' rather than the letter name, but that is quite acceptable for this task as he showed that he has a way to differentiate this letter from all the others.

Andrew knows a lot about how books work. He understands that books have a front and that they start on the first page.

He knows that the text is important for the story and not just the picture. He understands the concepts of first and last when we are talking about text in books. He knows that we start reading at

---

27   See http://readingrecovery.org/reading-recovery/teaching-children/observation-survey

the top left side of the page and we read left to right and then do a return – sweep to the next line and start on the left, again reading left to right. Andrew could almost match the words to his finger for pointing one-to-one, but was not quite able to do this accurately.

It is now the following month, and Andrew is able to accurately point one-to-one to words as he reads. If his finger 'gets ahead of his voice' he is able to go back again and 'make it match' as he reads.

Andrew can show a letter and a word, or two letters and two words, and does not confuse these. He knows what a period and a question mark are for when a person is reading.

Andrew can read several sight words, including: I, am, to, too, away, here, is, up, big, he, at, one, my, no. He can write several words, including: his name, mom, mommy, dad, daddy (although he has difficulty with b and d reversals), I, a, am, it, no, yes, too.

He is also able to listen to a little story (two sentences) and do his best to write it when it is said again, word by word, to him. He was able to 'hear and record' many sounds in words accurately. For example, he heard 'home' and wrote 'hom' which has all the sounds for that word.

In his Reading Recovery lessons, Andrew is writing one-sentence stories about topics he chooses. These are often about his pets. Andrew writes as much as he is able to independently, and I teach and support him to figure out words he doesn't know. I also write part of some words to support the writing process. I am teaching him writing strategies. During this time we also work on correct printing or letter formation.

Andrew is reading early Grade One books. I am reinforcing the reading strategies that he knows and am teaching him more reading strategies that are appropriate for his reading level. He loves books and loves to read, and this is such a strength.

I keep in close touch with his classroom teacher and the educational assistant and we work together to ensure that what Andrew is learning in the classroom is being transferred to his Reading Recovery lessons, and what he learns in Reading Recovery he is also transferring and using in the classroom.[28]

---

28 Permission received to reproduce this from the parents and teacher.

The CSP Spelling and Language Programme

This can be used in Year 1 and with whole-class teaching. Rhyme patterns, high frequency words and curriculum word banks are included in the programme. It can be suitable for Years 1–3 and the results seem very promising in developing spelling skills.[29]

THRASS (Teaching Handwriting, Reading and Spelling Skills)

This scheme was developed by Alan Davies (1996) and was made available for computers in 1997. It has become a very popular program internationally, for both teachers and parents. It is firmly based on multisensory principles and it has a helpful website. It displays a wide range of materials that are visually appealing and there are also musical activities associated with it, which can be very useful for early years.[30]

Toe by Toe

This is an extremely well-known and popular program. Keda Cowling worked on the scheme throughout her lengthy teaching experience (Cowling and Cowling 1998). It is delivered on a one-on-one basis and takes children to the foundations of phonics and works up from there. There is clear progression built into the program and this can be recorded by the child in his or her own Toe by Toe book. There are a great number of positive evaluations of Toe by Toe.[31]

Principles of programmes

Reid (2016a) suggests the following division below in relation to the type of intervention for children with dyslexia.

- *Individualised programmes:* These are usually highly structured, and can be seen as essentially free standing. They can form a central element of the overall strategy for teaching children with dyslexia or at risk of dyslexia. Most individualised

---

29 See www.interventionsforliteracy.org.uk/home/interventions/list-view/the-complete-spelling-programme

30 See www.thrass.co.uk

31 See www.toe-by-toe.co.uk

programmes incorporate some or all of the following principles and approaches:

- » multisensory, that is, uses all available senses simultaneously; this can be summed up in the phrase 'hear it, say it, see it and write it'

- » over-learning and automaticity – a lot of repetition

- » highly structured and usually phonically based

- » sequential and cumulative – follows a progression starting at the foundations of literacy.

- *Support approaches and strategies:* These may use the same principles as some of the individual programmes, but can be used more selectively by the teacher, thus making it possible to integrate them more easily within the normal activities of the curriculum.

- *Assisted learning techniques:* These can use many different methods, but a central essential component is the aspect of learning from others. These could therefore involve either peer or adult support and interaction, and utilise some of the principles of modelling.

- *Whole-class approaches:* These recognise that dyslexia is a whole-class and whole-school concern, and not just the responsibility of individual teachers. Such approaches require an established and accessible policy framework for consultancy, whole-school screening and monitoring of children's progress. Early identification is a further key aspect.

Number work

Some strategies for number work in children at risk of dyslexia include:

- learning challenging words visually

- numbering the steps to solving the problem

- giving instructions one step at a time

- teaching visualisation techniques such as highlighting and colour coding

- making visual facts cards for the properties of different shapes

- making number charts using different designs.

Resources that may be suitable for pre-school and early years

Reading

- *Posters:* They make a visual imprint on the child and because they are there for a long time the message in the poster will get through. This is particularly important for the child with dyslexia.

- *Labels:* It is important to label as many items as possible. This is again an over-learning technique as the child is exposed to the word all the time if it is used as a label.

- *Alphabet resources:* These are invaluable; although the child with dyslexia may know the alphabet they will receive over-learning using all sorts of resources. This helps with automaticity. For example, Activity Village has some excellent alphabet game ideas such as Alphabets in Scrapbooks, Alphabet Race, Alphabet Scrabble and Alphabet Trail.[32] These provide over-learning for the child with dyslexia, including simple activities such as Alphabet Shuffle, which involves shuffling a set of alphabet cards and then putting them back in order as quickly as possible. The child with dyslexia does not need to compete with others but can use this modality to help monitor their own progress and see how they can improve on their own speed.

- *Picture cards:* These need to be labelled, and it is important that the words are associated with the picture.

- *Letters:* Of any size and materials – wooden, plastic and cardboard. The idea is that the children experience the shape of the letter, so making the letters themselves would be excellent. This is the kinaesthetic experience that is so valuable for reinforcing learning. It is ideal for developing spelling.

---

32   See www.activityvillage.co.uk/alphabet-games

- *Computer apps:* A growing number of apps are now available and these will increase in years to come. The apps are interactive, colourful and visual, and ideal for young children with dyslexia.

- *Play sand:* This must be one of the most versatile and useful activities in the nursery/pre-school. So much can be done with a sand tray, such as alphabet skills.

- *Play-Doh:* This is good for fine motor manipulation, and can help writing skills. It can be a good group activity to make things together and is also good for social interaction.

- *Story cue cards/story telling cards:* These are excellent for retelling a story, but also for sequencing the narrative.

Resources grid

It is a good idea to develop a resources grid, as in the example in the appendix. This can act as an information resource for future reference for you and your colleagues. It can be added to as new publications appear. It is useful to add the date next to the resource, or have a separate column for the date.

Numeracy suggestions

There are many websites around that can be helpful for number work. One of the more useful ones includes a video by Steve Chinn (an internationally recognised maths specialist). His work and the film clip 'Maths Explained' is underpinned by Steve's research and experience, and research from leading experts from around the world.[33] It illustrates concepts simply and unlocks learning barriers, which children often experience with maths. The lessons also provide a solid foundation and the children work at their own pace.

Support strategies for maths and dyslexia

- Make the teaching multisensory with the use of age-appropriate concrete materials.

---

33   See www.stevechinn.co.uk/maths-explained.html

- Give clear worked examples as posters around the room and highlight signs, etc. in colour.

- Use maths puzzles – have a puzzle of the week and get the students to find puzzles to challenge the class.

- It is worth noting that poorer short-term memory, slower writing speeds and weaker knowledge of basic number facts will mean that those children with dyslexia will require more time to complete a given task.

- Paint/collage to develop the shapes of numbers and maths symbols.

- Number games of any sort can be excellent – iPad apps can be good for this.

- Shop, library, etc. – this can be a good exercise for organising and sorting out materials and objects, and is useful for practising counting.

- Tape measure, ruler, measuring cups, coins, clocks, watches – these are all good for measuring in a fun way.

- Scales/balance boards – these can help to develop the concept of weight and mass.

- An egg timer and stopwatch can help with the concept of time.

Developing language skills

It has already been noted that children with or at risk of dyslexia can have some language issues. Any form of activity that can help with talking and listening will be useful. These include:

- walkie talkies
- telephone tubes
- voice recorders
- songs
- story telling
- dressing-up costumes

- play telephones
- dramatic play area
- Wendy house.

Writing and pre-writing skills

Writing and pre-writing skills both need to be planned. It is also a good idea to ensure that the resources the child may need are available at this stage:

- any activity using fine motor skills
- clipboards for drawing and scribbling
- sign-in book to use as a model for writing name
- writing table
- picture books
- clay and other materials.

Handwriting – some points to consider

It is also a good idea to ensure that the child has the correct posture and pencil grip prior to writing. There are many points worth considering with writing and some of these are shown below:

- hand dominance
- pencil grip
- posture
- paper position
- pressure on paper
- wrist movement
- letter formation
- left to right orientation
- reversals of letters

- spacing

- letter size, formation consistency

- style – joins in letters

- speed

- fatigue factors.

Movement and coordination

It is also a good idea to observe the child's abilities in activities that require coordination as well as gross motor activities, such as skipping and running. Other activities include:

- balancing

- climbing

- control over movement activities, such as hopping, skipping

- soft play activities

- bikes and trikes.

Observation to support teaching

Behaviour to be observed	Possible responses	Possible interventions
Attention	Short attention span when listening	Short tasks with frequent breaks
Organisation	Keeps losing items – not well-organised	Needs structure – guidance and strategies to help with organisation
Sequencing	Not able to put things in order, carry out instructions in order	Make lists, keep instructions short, colour code
Interaction	Preferred interaction – one-to-one? Small groups? Whole class?	Try to ensure there is a balance of one-to-one, small group and class work

Expressive language	Meaning not accurately conveyed	Provide key points when discussing; do not ask open-ended questions; follow up answers with more specific questions
Are responses spontaneous or prompted?	Needs a lot of encouragement to respond	Identify strengths and allow the child to use these in different tasks
How does the child comprehend information?	Needs a lot of repetition	Use over-learning but try to make it varied so it is not too repetitive
What type of cues most readily facilitate comprehension?	Needs a lot of visual cues	Ensure opportunities for illustrating answer – space out work on worksheets, as visual image is important
What type of instructions are most easily understood – written, oral, visual?	Has difficulty with oral instructions	Ensure instructions are understood – need to be reinforced verbally
How readily can knowledge be transferred to other areas?	Has difficulty in knowing how to make connections with previous knowledge	Needs a structure showing how new learning applies to previous learning
Reading preferences – aloud, silent?	Has difficulty in reading aloud	Minimise reading aloud in front of class
Type of errors	Note the type of errors he or she makes when reading aloud	See the section on miscue analysis and the interpretation of reading errors (see page 53)
Difficulties in auditory discrimination	Inability to hear consonant sounds in initial, medial or final position	Use paired reading as it provides both auditory and visual feedback to the learner
Motivation level? Does the child take the initiative?	Reluctant to take initiative – needs a lot of prompting and is not highly motivated	Encourage group work where responsibility is delegated so that everyone has a turn to be in charge

Behaviour to be observed	Possible responses	Possible interventions
How is motivation increased? What kind of prompting and cueing is necessary?	Working with others seems to help	Make sure the group he or she is in is a positive experience. Experiment until you get the right group dynamics
To what extent does the child take responsibility for own learning?	Reluctant to do this – needs a lot of coaxing, otherwise waits for the teacher to provide instructions	Meet the child halfway – provide a lead in and then get him or her to finish it, but ensure there is constant monitoring
Level of self-concept?	Seems to have a low level of self-concept	Look for ways of giving the child some responsibility for his or her own learning – identify the strengths and highlight these, try to ensure that tasks are achievable
What tasks are more likely to be tackled with confidence?	Avoids writing but seems to be confident in practical tasks	Team up with writing buddy – balance writing with tactile and kinaesthetic tasks
Is the child relaxed when learning?	Seems a bit stressed at times	Avoid too much pressure, allow more time for tasks – try to ensure that the learner manages to complete all tasks and does not fall behind
What is the child's learning preferences?	Seems to be visual and kinaesthetic	Ensure that learning is experiential and there are a lot of visuals

Social and emotional development

Confidence, social awareness and self-esteem can be developed though 'circle time' activities, such as turn-taking, group discussion and role-play, where children have to undertake sharing and problem-solving activities together (see page 114). Jenny Mosley's work is well known, and many of the activities provided on her website can be helpful.[34]

Other activities to meet individual needs

- Any kind of activity game.
- Being able to talk confidently about feelings and behaviour.
- Games and activities to develop self-confidence.
- Developing listening skills – circle time can also be good for this.
- Introducing values education, such as caring for the community.
- Ensuring effective peer friendships are possible.
- Safety activities and role-play based on these.
- Any form of role-play activity or game.
- Sensory play and preferably in teams.
- Construction activities like LEGO®.

Reid and Green (2008, 2016) indicate that the following general points should be considered:

- Use charts and diagrams to highlight the bigger picture of what is being taught.
- Use mime and gesture to help the kinaesthetic learner, that is, the learner who prefers to learn through active involvement and experience. For example, drama is a good type of kinaesthetic activity.
- Add pictures to text.
- Use colour to highlight key words.
- Label diagrams and charts.
- Use games to consolidate vocabulary.

---

34   See www.circle-time.co.uk/site/things_to_try/lesson_plans

- Make packs of pocket-size cards of important words.

- Use different colours for different purposes.

- Combine listening and reading by providing text and tape.

- Use Mind Maps® and spidergrams.

- Present information in small amounts with frequent opportunities for repetition and revision.

There are good examples of pre-school reading worksheets and printables at Education.com[35] including Letter Sounds, Beginning Sounds, Q is for...? U is for...?, All About the Letter F, Letter Sounds Y, Pre-Kindergarten Sight Words and many more. These are colourful and informative and well-designed posters. Again these are ideal for the learner with dyslexia as they are a constant reinforcement of the teaching point.

Concluding thoughts

This chapter has looked at a range of approaches and programmes. There is no one approach or strategy that is suitable for all children at risk of dyslexia or indeed diagnosed with dyslexia. It is important to be aware of a number of established strategies and, very importantly, the underlying principles that support these strategies.

For that reason the research and original sources have been included in this chapter. It is important, of course, to appreciate that locating approaches and strategies to meet individual needs is only part of the response. It is also important to consider the curriculum and classroom and school context. These are discussed in the following chapter, and without doubt these key factors interplay – an effective combination of these will more likely result in a successful outcome.

---

35   See www.education.com/worksheets/preschool/reading/

Chapter 5

Intervention Approaches
Meeting Classroom Needs

This chapter focuses on classroom and nursery approaches that can be useful for those children at risk of dyslexia. This includes policies and practices for pre-school and early years intervention, planning for learning, target setting and monitoring and reviewing progress.

Literacy-rich pre-school environment

The pre-school years are vital, and in fact, the infant years before the child is 3 years old is also a key period for developing early literacy skills.

Gustaffsson, Hansen and Rosén (2011), from the University of Gothenburg in Sweden, indicated that one of the more stable and consistently observed phenomena in education is the impact of the student's home background on achievement. From this it follows that the pre-reading skills and existence of a literacy-rich home environment are important.

Reid *et al.* (2004) reported on some very promising examples from Scotland stemming from the results of a government-supported research project, *Scotland-wide Audit of Education Authority Early Years Policies and Provision Regarding Specific Learning Difficulties (SpLD) and Dyslexia*. The quote below highlights some valuable points that can be readily utilised by all:

> The authority indicated that they had a clear commitment to identifying children with dyslexia as early as possible. They saw the Pre-School Home Visiting Service as a valuable resource that

was available to families from the start of a child's life. This service provided support to parents and practical advice about pre-school services best suited to their child's needs. In addition this service supported children in transition from home to pre-school setting and across services by providing advice and guidance for staff about the child's learning needs and preferences and about strategies which will work well with that child. The Pre-School Home Visiting Service works closely with a range of education and health professionals in order to establish a shared all round assessment of children's learning needs.

This approach is the type of commitment that is required to ensure that children at risk of dyslexia are identified as early as possible. The key points in this document are the clear commitment to identifying dyslexia as early as possible and the home visiting service that can enable the transition from home to nursery and inform staff of the best approaches and strategies to use for any particular child. These points can be integrated into any system in order to ensure early identification.

Schools as barriers

Weedon (2016), however, argues that schools can be instrumental in creating barriers and are therefore complicit in a 'social construction' of disability. He argues that through necessity the early school environment places much emphasis on the acquisition of core literacy and numeracy skills – and for the children at risk of dyslexia this may be something that they cannot do quite as easily as would be expected. He suggests that the happy pre-school child becomes perhaps less happy in early primary school due to these factors and expectations.

Dealing with the barriers

A major initiative in the Republic of Ireland can be seen in the *Report of the Task Force on Dyslexia* (Department of Education and Skills (Ireland) 2001). Although this was some time ago now, it was a far-reaching comprehensive government report and the result of the deliberations of a government-appointed task force. The Task Force received 399 written submissions from individuals, educational institutions and organisations, and 896 oral submissions from individuals by telephone. The report noted that parents in particular shared their views and frustrations, and confirmed that they have first-hand experience of their children's learning difficulties arising from dyslexia. It is important to take the parents' perspective into account as they very likely have the most experience of the type of difficulties and strengths the child experiences. The report also showed clear indicators of dyslexia for different age groups – 3–5, 5–7, 7–12 and 12+. This is a strong commitment to identifying dyslexia at an early age, and it is commendable that this was one of the first reports of this kind to be produced.

Suggestions for linking assessment with intervention

It has already been established in earlier chapters that dyslexia is a difficulty or difference with the processing of information. There are three areas to information processing: input, cognition (processing) and output. Below are some suggestions on dealing with this difficulty.

Input

- Present new information in small steps – this will ensure that the short-term memory does not become overloaded with information before the new information is fully consolidated.

- New material will need to be repeatedly presented through over-learning. This does not mean that the repetition should be in the same form; rather it is important that it should be varied, using as wide a range of materials and strategies as possible. This can be achieved through using the facilities and resources at the pre-school stage.

- It is a good idea to present the key points at the initial stage of learning new material. This helps to provide a framework for the new material and can help in relating new information to previous knowledge.

- Even young children will have a preferred learning style. They may have visual, auditory, kinaesthetic or tactile preferences. These can be important in relation to how information is presented. Most children can adapt to different forms of presentation, but children with dyslexia can find this more difficult.

- Find out what the child's preferred modality is and use this with new learning so he or she can understand and then you can use other modalities.

Cognition

- Try to relate new information to previous knowledge. This ensures that concepts are developed and the child can place the information into a learning framework or schema. Many children such as those with dyslexia may need some support to develop a schema.

- Successful learning is often due to how information is organised. Group information together and show the connection between the two.

Output

- Young children with dyslexia can have a word-finding difficulty and may have difficulties in relating exactly what they mean. This can be overcome by providing them with these key points or words at the beginning stage of learning the new material. Additionally they can acquire skills in this by practising repeating what they have done.

Support through communication and exchange

Many national and international organisations associated with dyslexia now have internet-based forums or social media pages where practitioners can exchange ideas. See, for example, Learning Works®[1] and the Helen Arkell Dyslexia Centre Facebook page.[2] Many also carry out their own research and develop their own programmes. See,

---

1   See www.learning-works.org.uk
2   See www.facebook.com/pages/Helen-Arkell-Dyslexia-Centre/113209298712058

for example, Dyslexia Action *Units of Sound* Version 6 (2014), the Helen Arkell Dyslexia Centre's *Anyone Can Spell It* (Fletcher and Caplan 2014), the *Helen Arkell Spelling Test Version 2* (Caplan *et al.* 2012), and internationally the International Dyslexia Association (IDA)[3] and the Centre for Child Education and Teaching (CCET) in Kuwait.[4] The Institute for Child Education and Psychology (ICEP) (Europe) has a wide range of university-accredited training programmes that are well-researched, based on practical approaches with supporting theoretical perspectives.[5]

Curriculum support: Meeting needs through policy

Curriculum for Excellence (Scotland)[6]

In Scotland the key initiative in relation to the broad range of support can be seen in the Curriculum for Excellence document. This was introduced to raise the standards of learning and teaching for all 3–18-year-olds. It aims to help prepare children and young people with the knowledge and skills they need in a fast-changing world. Education authorities therefore follow the Curriculum for Excellence programme in all schools and pre-school establishments.[7]

Essentially Curriculum for Excellence is designed to achieve a transformation in education in Scotland by providing a coherent, more flexible and enriched curriculum from 3 to 18. The curriculum includes the totality of experiences that are planned for children and young people through their education, wherever they are being educated. One of the key elements of this is the 'Building your Curriculum' process that was developed to help schools and centres review their curriculum structures and to develop their own 'take' of the curriculum. It therefore promotes flexibility within the targets set by the document.

One of the bonus points of this for young children is that it gives them the opportunity for assuming some responsibility for their learning and practice in making choices. This was highlighted during

---

3   See http://dyslexiaida.org

4   See www.ccetkuwait.org

5   See www.icepe.ie and www.icepe.co.uk

6   See www.educationscotland.gov.uk/learningandteaching/thecurriculum/whatis curriculumforexcellence

7   West Lothian Council provides one example. See www.westlothian.gov.uk/ article/2236/Curriculum-for-Excellence

an HM Inspectorate of Education inspection in 2014 at Victoria Quay Nursery, which is part of North Edinburgh Childcare Enterprise Ltd. The idea is to help children express their own views, which can be through play, the choice of resources and activities as well as established activities such as circle time. This can be beneficial for children with dyslexia as it not only involves reading but also discussion, which they can usually do very well.

Similarly, an innovative approach can be seen in the approaches to planning and assessment at Monkton Primary School Nursery class in South Ayrshire.[8] The idea was to help children understand themselves as learners, and the staff then spent less time on planning activities and more time interacting with children during play activities. They renamed this 'the learning journey' so the emphasis was less on what they did and more on what they had learned. This is an excellent proposal for preventing children with dyslexia from experiencing failure. The emphasis is on what they can do and not on what they cannot do. The key thing is that children became more aware of what they were learning and how they were doing it. The staff reported that children were now more engaged in learning and initiated some innovative ideas. A mud kitchen with real materials and utensils was created and they also learned how to learn more effectively by listening and observing other children, minimising any competitive element.

Special Educational Needs and Disability Code of Practice 0–25

In England and Wales the *SEND Code of Practice 0–25 Years* (DfE and DH 2014b) provides guidance on planning for learning and reviewing progress at the pre-school stage as well as the early years of primary. The document emphasises the need to:

- *Assess:* This involves carrying out an analysis of the child's needs, which should be done in conjunction with the parents. The initial assessment should be reviewed regularly, but if there is no progress, a fuller specialist assessment should take place. This is promising as, using this framework, the teacher would very likely be able to spot potentially dyslexic children.

---

8   See https://education.gov.scot/improvement/Pages/elc6childrensljmonkton.aspx

- *Plan:* This is essentially to do with the outcomes that are proposed and the type of support the child needs. Evidence of effectiveness in the approaches to be used is the key here. It also provides an opportunity to identify areas for further staff development.

- *Do:* This would involve the early years practitioner in conjunction with the SENCo to oversee the implementation of the programme that is to be put in place. It is also an opportunity for the SENCo to advise further on the intervention.

- *Review:* This is an important stage as it looks at the effectiveness of the support and the progress the child has made so far. It is important that parents are fully involved and aware of the next steps.

There are a considerable amount of resources that can help in the 'Do' category, and many can be downloaded either free or at a low cost from a number of websites. The TES website is particularly useful. For example, 'Writing Words from Pictures' for beginning writers (Hislop 2014) is a superb example of a colourful and simple procedure that can provide a step-by-step programme for children who may be dyslexic. The children learn to write by sounding out, and the worksheets include CVC words, short and long vowel sounds, and digraphs and blends. Hislop also has excellent materials on numbers (using number posters) and Oxford Word Bingo (sight words), which involves making sets of 20 words and laminating them so that they can be used in games.

For children at risk of dyslexia the ability to rhyme may be quite difficult. Nursery rhymes are an excellent way of teaching some essential prerequisites of reading. These include sounds and word discrimination, blending and phoneme manipulation, all of which children with dyslexia are likely to have difficulty with.

Primary Resources is also a very useful website for early years,[9] and has activities on nursery and early years planning, as well as a range of activities in the Welsh medium.[10]

Crossbow Education is one of the most prolific stockists of materials that will keep children interested in the activity. For example,

---

9   See www.primaryresources.co.uk/foundation/foundation.htm

10   See www.primaryresources.co.uk/welsh/welsh.htm

for phonics and spelling they have short and long vowel games, magnetic foam letters and other games and activities including specific materials to help with the visual discrimination of words such as eye-level rulers and pencil grips to help with writing.[11]

Early Years: Guide to the 0 to 25 SEND Code of Practice

One of the key specifications in this guide (DfE 2014b) relates to collaboration, which is essential in the pre-school area. The aim is to achieve greater collaboration between education, health and social care. The guide also acknowledges that too many children do not get the support they need early enough, and the support they receive is not sufficiently focused enough to help them meet their goals. Although this particular document has no statutory basis, it does provide guidance to early years providers, and should be looked at in the context of the Children and Families Act 2014. There is a significant emphasis on working with families and parents, removing the barriers to learning and developing and maintaining inclusive practices. There is also an emphasis on ensuring that the SENCo covers the early years to ensure SEN support is available.

In terms of 'early years outcomes', a range of exemplification materials is provided.[12] These focus on listening and attention, understanding, speaking, moving and handling, health and self-care, self-confidence and self-awareness, managing feelings and behaviour, making relationships, reading, writing, numbers, shapes, space and measures, people and communities, technology, media, investigation and being imaginative. These are excellent exemplars, well illustrated and relevant. This is a very useful document and very accessible.

Reggio Emilia approach[13]

Amy Sussna Klein (2009) comments very positively on the popular Reggio Emilia approach. It has won much support from early years practitioners and educationalists, and is based on the system used in Reggio Emilia, a small town of about 130,000 people in

---

11   See www.crossboweducation.com
12   See www.gov.uk/government/publications/eyfs-profile-exemplification-materials
13   See www.reggiochildren.it

Northern Italy. Klein comments that in 1991 *Newsweek* magazine noted that the system of 33 infant/toddler schools and pre-schools in Reggio Emilia were among the ten best school systems in the world. Klein suggests that over the last 35 years the approach has been broadened to incorporate constructivist theory, and many practitioners have applauded the results. Essentially, constructivist theory refers to learning by doing, and the construction of knowledge is based on the child's own interests and interpretation of the world. The basis of learning in the Reggio Emilia system is exploration and discovery and the development of the child's unique skills and talents.

Klein comments that the main approaches of Reggio Emilia are cooperation and collaboration; valuing social learning; ensuring connections between families, schools and the community; long-term projects; emphasis on portfolios; the creation of a tranquil but stimulating environment conducive to learning; and the use of flow charts to explain what happened before, what is being discussed now and what predictions can be made for what may emerge (the future).

The Reggio Emilia approach is built on a unique infrastructure – not too unlike the Montessori approach – and relationships are important. It has many supporters and is now practised internationally.

Some key factors on early education

The learning context relates to the classroom or nursery environment, the type of provision and the teaching situation as well as whole-school factors such as school ethos and degree of culture.

Automaticity

Automaticity develops from long practice under consistent conditions, and underpins almost all of our highly practised skills, from speech to walking to arithmetic. One of the critical aspects of learning a skill is to make it automatic, so that it can be done fluently without thinking about it. By adulthood, most skills – walking, talking, reading – are so deeply over-learned that we no longer have any insight into how we acquired them.

Automatisation is a key requirement for reading, and Fawcett and Nicolson (2008) suggest that there is extensive evidence that dyslexic children, even when reading well, are less fluent, requiring more time and effort to read than a non-dyslexic child of the same reading age.

There is a considerable body of evidence that shows that strategies for teaching reading and writing skills to dyslexic children should be multisensory and phonic-based, and that this type of teaching can benefit most children in the early stages (Rose 2009).

Additionally, it is a well-established view that dyslexic children require considerable over-learning to achieve automaticity. Automaticity is important for the learning of any skill (Everatt and Reid 2009), but it is particularly important for children with dyslexia as there is evidence (see Fawcett 2002; Fawcett and Nicolson 2008) that dyslexic children have a dyslexia automatisation deficit – the 'DAD hypothesis' (Nicolson and Fawcett 1990). This means that children with dyslexia will require additional time to develop automaticity in any skill, but particularly in literacy, and this needs to be considered in a teaching programme.

Structure

A structure includes a progression that should be logical and in small steps and, importantly, the links between the steps should be clear and explicit.

As well as the additional time factors needed to acquire automaticity, it is also important to develop a carefully planned structure for a teaching programme that takes automaticity into account. A structure requires much more than detailing the teaching order of the points that children must learn; it should also involve the learning experiences provided to the student. For example, Crombie (2002, 2016) suggests that if a child requires to spell a word, but is unaware of the order of the sounds being heard, a jumbling of letters will likely occur unless visual memory can compensate for this weakness. Teaching the child to repeat words, while listening to the order of the sounds, is, according to Crombie (2002), time well spent. This is particularly important as children with dyslexic difficulties do not often automatically pick up the order of sounds. This means that the interaction between teacher and student is important, and some children need to be taught before they can learn a particular skill or sequence.

Over-learning

Over-learning is important in order to consolidate new and existing learning. Children with dyslexia will take longer to consistently use new learning or to read or recognise letters and sounds without hesitation. In order to achieve automaticity it is important that over-learning follows some principles:

- The golden rule for teaching children with dyslexia is to use a range of *multisensory* methods – auditory, visual, kinaesthetic (experiential) and tactile (touch and sensation).

- Learning should be active (doing) and interactive (discussing and working with others), as well as incorporating elements of all the modalities above – auditory, visual, kinaesthetic and tactile.

- Metacognitive – although metacognition is usually seen as part of a programme for older children, there is no reason why it cannot be used for younger children as well. Essentially, metacognition involves thinking about thinking, and encourages the learner to self-question how he or she arrived at a particular response.

English as an Additional Language (EAL) learners

Coffield *et al.* (2008) argue that irrespective of home language it is important to ensure that the needs of *individual* children are not overlooked, and particularly to bear in mind that the difficulties children with dyslexia experience are not all the same. It cannot be assumed that putting one or two strategies into place that are generally considered suitable for children with dyslexia will suffice when it comes to meeting the range of educational and emotional needs that these pupils might have – one size does not necessarily fit all.

This area is also dealt with in Chapter 9, but it is also important to refer to it here. Philips, Kelly and Symes (2013) argue that in the case of EAL children who are dyslexic, it is important to take into account that proficiency in *both* first language and English can aid conceptual understanding and therefore comprehension. Siegel reinforces this point (2016).

Response to Intervention (RTI) approach

Findings from numerous research studies indicate that many young children in the US, particularly those from low SES backgrounds, begin school at risk for reading failure because of weak oral language skills (Bardige 2005; Brown and Bogard 2007; Neuman 2006). As an example, in their seminal study Hart and Risley (2003) found that by age 3, children who came from higher SES families had vocabularies twice the size of those coming from lower SES families. This difference in vocabulary development was predictive of the children's performance on language and literacy measures through 3rd grade, with children from higher SES families continuing to outperform their peers from lower SES families.

Similarly, data reported from the US Department of Education's Early Childhood Longitudinal Study, Kindergarten cohort (ECLS-K) on more than 20,000 children from across the US provides additional evidence of the negative impact this achievement gap has on the reading performance of both low SES and culturally and linguistically diverse children into 5th grade (Princiotta, Flanagan and Hausken 2006). While the under-achievement that many of these children experience may be attributed to dyslexia, many of them struggle with reading because of poor oral language skills. Early identification of reading difficulty along with targeted, research-based interventions can improve children's chances of becoming more effective readers (Lamy, Barnett and Jung 2005; Lynch 2007).

The RTI process may be an effective mechanism for both identifying children who struggle to acquire reading skills and implementing appropriate interventions to help them succeed in school. Identification of dyslexia has been problematic as it is often based on a 'discrepancy', 'wait-to-fail' model rather than a prevention model. The 2004 reauthorisation of Individuals with Disabilities Act, the US law that addresses the educational needs of children with disabilities from birth to the age of 21, allowed states to use RTI processes to identify and intervene on behalf of students performing below the expected level of achievement. In addition, it encourages the development of Early Intervening Services (EIS). These two concepts have resulted in general and special education being more closely aligned. Alexa Posny, Director of the US Office of Special Education Programs (OSEP), stated, 'RTI and EIS are absolutely the future of education

– not the future of special education, but of education' (quoted in Burdette 2007, p.3). The RTI approach is particularly encouraging in the field of early childhood education because it promotes child-centred instruction and effectively deals with the problems inherent in the 'wait-to-fail' model.

There are many variations of RTI, and perhaps this is its strength as it can be tailored to local requirements, local, context and local needs. Coleman, Buysse and Neitzel (2006) created an RTI process for pre-school children called 'Recognition and Response' that includes four essential components: an intervention hierarchy; screening, assessment and progress monitoring; research-based curriculum, instruction and focused interventions; and a collaborative problem-solving process for decision-making. Essentially this can make early years classrooms language and literacy-rich environments and promote language skills and the idea of learning how to learn (Mashburn *et al.* 2008; Pianta and Hadden 2008).

The specific language-based skills young children need to acquire through their pre-school experience that can form the basis of early intervention such as RTI are:

- oral expressive and receptive language skills that support vocabulary development

- syntactic development and inferential thinking

- print awareness

- phonological awareness skills such as rhyming, alliteration, word and syllable segmentation and phoneme awareness

- alphabet knowledge.

Knight *et al.* (2009) argue that with effective universal screening, progress monitoring and early referral for diagnosis as part of an RTI process, children with dyslexia may be more likely to be identified early and appropriately. Although dyslexia cannot be cured, its severity can be ameliorated by early intervention targeted to address the specific difficulties the student encounters.

Multiskill intervention

Fawcett, Lee and Nicolson (2014) studied the sustained benefits of multiskill intervention for pre-school children at risk of literacy difficulties. In their study the intervention group had small group support (15-minute sessions twice weekly for ten weeks) while the control group experienced the standard nursery intervention. The intervention comprised four 'streams' – language and phonics, memory (auditory and visual), gross motor skills (balance, imitation and catching) and fine motor skills (pegboard, tool use and fine pencil work). Both groups performed equivalently at pre-test. An immediate post-test showed mean standard score improvement for the intervention group (93.1 to 106.2) in contrast with the control group (96.9 to 98.5). This means that significantly greater improvements occurred for gross motor skill, memory and phonology including rhyming. After 18 months, sustained improvements were found in memory, a key predictor of success in early learning, as well as in gross motor skills. The results suggested that a balanced, multiskill intervention might be particularly effective for pre-school children.

Guidelines for cost-effective nursery screening and intervention emerged from this study which include the administration of short age-normed screening tests designed for this age group, followed by explicit small group teaching of language and motor skills over a short time frame, with further individual targeted intervention for children who do not accelerate. This is very promising, and can be readily implemented.

Problem to solution approach

Came (2007) has developed a strategy that is firmly embedded in curriculum assessment and intervention. Although it can be used throughout the school it can also be contextualised for the early years. It is based on the idea of finding out what the problem is, locating the evidence, that is, how we know there is a problem, planning for action (the priorities, action), and the intervention – this is a cyclical process so there are built-in reviews and re-assessment to find out if there is still a problem (see page 50).

Concluding thoughts

A number of important points can be drawn from this and the previous chapter. These include the point that no one method or strategy is suitable for all children with dyslexia. For that reason it is necessary to have a range of methods and strategies as long as they meet the established criteria for children with dyslexia – for example, they must be multisensory, offer step-by-step progression and include a great deal of over-learning.

At the same time it is important that the context, the child's background and the curriculum needs are all taken into account. It is important that the child feels comfortable in the mainstream class, and the teaching and resources selected can help maintain motivation. A differentiated, step-by-step process helps the child achieve some success, and success in any form is essential at this stage in the child's education.

Chapter 6

Emotional and Social Issues and Motivation

This chapter looks at emotional and social issues and how to deal with these in the nursery and classroom context in a one-to-one situation and also in a group setting.

Social learning

Learning can be fun and for very young children, it usually is! All children are, however, quite different, and we need to acknowledge individual differences. This means that some learners may want to work in groups while others may opt to be by themselves when learning. It is important to acknowledge these individual social differences and not to misconstrue these as being in any way a sign of deviance or a disability. At the same time, some young children find the idea of learning in isolation quite traumatic and it can reduce motivation. For many young children learning is a social experience. This can give them emotional security. Both social and emotional factors are instrumental in effective learning.

Any group task can facilitate social learning but often it will have to be monitored to ensure that all children are involved. This type of activity can promote a number of key learning factors that can be helpful for all children, but will also benefit those at risk of dyslexia. Social learning can promote turn-taking, developing a positive attitude to others as well as promoting a positive self-concept.

Drama is a good example of social learning and young children usually enjoy this. The young child at risk of dyslexia can become totally involved, and it is important that he or she does not get a slot in the drama that might expose their challenges with reading or timing. They can be very creative and may come up with some novel and fascinating ideas. As drama involves role-play and pretend play, again, this can feed into the young child's imagination and develop their creative side. It is something that the young person with dyslexia can excel in. It is also good to encourage improvisation as this means that the child doesn't have to remember lengthy lines or scripts.

Songs and recitals are also good, such as making up their own songs – the children have some leeway with the words and actions, and this prevents the embarrassment of young children with dyslexia not being able to remember the words. Performing the songs can provide a real boost to motivation and the involvement of all in the learning task.

'Feeling good' in learning

The child has to want to learn, and needs to feel good within him or herself. It is worthwhile taking time to ensure that the child is emotionally ready for the task. Some young children can feel totally swamped and overwhelmed by a task and may not have the language skills to articulate this. It might be important to talk this through with them before they proceed. Try the Double F, P and R formula (Reid 2007):

- *Feelings:* Ask how the child feels about doing the task.

- *Feedback:* Feed back to the child what he or she has already achieved towards doing the task.

- *Perspective:* Put in perspective what the child has to achieve.

- *Process:* Together with the child talk through the process – indicate clearly what has to be done first and then second.

- *Reasons:* Identify the reasons for any feelings of being overwhelmed and why this should be the case.

- *Re-align:* This is about goals and expectations – re-align jointly with the child some suggested goals that can be achieved.

Learning environment

The child has to feel comfortable in the environment and this may not be too obvious. Most children have little awareness of the best environment for them to learn effectively, which is not surprising since children at school usually have very little choice over their learning environment. It is important therefore to give children some options. This can include wall displays, colour, organisation of desks, seating arrangements, scope for movement, as well as the level of activity and group learning.

The *Wiltshire Early Years SENCO Toolbox* (2009) highlights the importance of ensuring that the environment is right and appropriate for the child who may have some social and emotional sensitivity. The toolbox indicates that it is important to be aware of aspects in the learning environment that may be fascinating and stimulating, but also those aspects that can promote anxiety and be worrying for the child. For example, a favourite book within sight can be positive, but a flickering light or computer screen may have an negative impact. It is also important to keep the workspace as uncluttered as possible. It is important that the child has scope for moving around the classroom, and also that they know where resources that they are permitted to use are and that they are accessible. They should be encouraged to access their own materials when appropriate.

Developing emotional awareness

Emotional development is important for the process of learning and the eventual success of a task. It is worthwhile spending class time on developing emotional security and helping children become aware of their emotional feelings. These can then be related to the actual task – for example, how they feel about doing a certain task and why they feel like that. The development of emotions can be seen at three levels: cognitive – how people think; physiological – the current state of bodily health and wellbeing; and affective – which relates to their understanding and awareness of their own and other people's emotions.

These may seem quite advanced for a young child, but it is important even at this young age to help children become aware of their own and other people's feelings. This can also help to develop empathy and eventually lead to a good sense of value and moral sense of right and wrong. The child with dyslexia should be able to participate in this type of activity and likewise the rest of the class in order to increase their awareness of the concept of differences and tolerance.

Risk assessment

As indicated above, Wiltshire County Council in the UK have developed an excellent early years SENCo toolbox that includes many strategies in the social and emotional area. Although it is mainly geared to children on the autistic spectrum and those with social and communication difficulties, it does contain some excellent tips that can be used across the board. It makes the important point of conducting a risk assessment, particularly in view of the unpredictability of these children. This is pertinent in outdoor activities, and Wiltshire County Council emphasises that it is important to have a back-up plan for a situation where a child can become over-anxious, for example, somewhere safe for them to retreat to if it becomes too much for them.

The SENCo toolbox provides some useful tips such as missing out unnecessary words in speech because the child may have processing speed difficulties, which means he or she can be slower in some social situations. This can also apply to children at risk of dyslexia who may also have processing speed difficulties. It is also important to recognise that a response may be longer in coming and the child will need more time to respond to questions in social situations.

The toolbox also emphasises the need to use positive rather than negative instructions. It might be useful to minimise the use of the word 'don't' but to reframe the instruction or command by saying what you want them to do instead.

Emotional literacy and emotional intelligence

Emotional literacy is essentially being emotionally aware, that is, being aware of one's emotions and the feelings of others. According to Killick (2005, p.14), emotional literacy provides 'a way of increasing the space that exists between feelings and actions'. Killick argues that this can be linked to emotional intelligence. Both relate to the capacity of an individual (and groups) to perceive, understand and manage emotions in oneself and relating to others. This is very important for social learning.

To have any real impact on the education and lives of children, emotional literacy therefore has to be fully absorbed and included into a whole-school ethos. Killick suggests that 'emotional literate children will have greater resilience to emotional problems' (2005, p.5), and it is often the case that emotional problems underlie the behaviour problems that are seen in the classroom.

Killick suggests that there are five pathways to emotional intelligence: self-awareness, self-regulation, motivation, empathy and social competence. These are all necessary for the development of emotional wellbeing and emotional literacy.

To ensure that schools have an ethos that is conducive to emotional literacy, factors such as organisational climate, organisational change, bullying, teacher stress, circle time communication, motivation, feedback, thinking skills, developing interpersonal skills and the role of reflection are all crucial. All these can be included in the nursery and early years classes. Again, these will be very helpful to the young child with dyslexia.

The checklist below gives an indication of the factors that are instrumental in emotional literacy, and how to identify if this is a priority area for the child.

Emotional literacy preparedness checklist

- ✓ Does the child show any stress signs?
- ✓ Can the child be left to work independently?
- ✓ Can the child persist with the task or will he or she require a lot of monitoring?
- ✓ Can the child only work for short periods?
- ✓ Does the child require constant reassurance?
- ✓ Is the child aware of the needs of others?

This can serve as a monitoring sheet to ascertain if the child is emotionally ready for the task. It may be necessary to do some preparatory work on the child's emotional wellbeing before he or she can work independently on it. It is also worth noting, as indicated earlier, that emotional literacy is a whole-school responsibility.

Children may well develop emotional literacy in one class, but if they are in a school that does not have an emotional literacy ethos, the gains may be lost.

Stress and learning

It is important to consider that even very young children can experience some stress and anxiety in the learning situation. There is a wide range of reasons why children can experience stress, which includes:

- *State of mind:* Some children are more prone and more vulnerable to stress than others. Trigger factors that can result in stress can therefore be quite different for different children. Some can seem quite mild and inconsequential, but for the child they are very real.

- *Worry/anxiety:* It is important to be aware that young children can worry about things that seem to the adult to be irrelevant. It is important to take all children's anxieties seriously.

- *Social reasons:* School is a social institution, but some children find it difficult to fit in, and the readjustment from home to school or from nursery to primary can be quite traumatic. This may result in a degree of social isolation and can be a source of unhappiness for many children.

- *Family reasons:* Families and carers occupy the central role in children's lives. If things go wrong or changes are made to the family life in whatever way, this can have an upsetting affect on some children. Much depends on how the change is handled and the quality and nature of the relationships they have with their parents or carers, which is why it is important to ensure that there are good links between home and school.

- *Learning to learn:* School can be a competitive institution. This is fine as it can stretch children to achieve, but at the same time it can demoralise some children who have difficulty in achieving. This may be the case with young children at risk of dyslexia. They may not have mastered the learning process and have little idea of how to tackle a problem or task. This is why they need a great deal of monitoring and guidance.

It is important that they are eventually encouraged to become independent learners, but it can take many years for them to achieve this.

- *School friendships:* Peer group friendships are very important to children. A breakdown in these can be the main source of unhappiness at school for some children. This should not be taken lightly and activities such as circle time[1] can help to develop peer group friendships and understanding. Mosley's (1996) website contains excellent materials to promote a positive classroom ethos and build emotional strength in young children. Her *Quality Circle Time* model is a whole-school approach and can be used effectively for early years settings as well as primary and secondary schools. Circle time can:

  » improve social skills and positive relationships

  » encourage positive behaviour and a caring and respectful ethos

  » help children develop their self-esteem and self-confidence

  » support the emotional wellbeing of children

  » create calm, happy lunchtimes and playtimes with lunchtime games and activities

  » promote the social and emotional development and creativity of children.

  All these points can be extremely beneficial for young children at risk of dyslexia.

- *Unrealistic expectations:* It is very important for young children that expectations are not too ambitious. This can include family, school and curricular expectations, and can, in fact, be one of the main causes of failure in early years. It is important that expectations, both from the children and the teacher's viewpoint, are seen to be flexible and in keeping with what that particular child can realistically achieve. There is now a move afoot in most countries to have set targets that children

---

1   See www.circle-time.co.uk

should achieve at certain ages. This is the type of policy that can put unnecessary pressure on the teacher and subsequently the child. The key aspect to managing expectations relates to ensuring that tasks are sufficiently differentiated to ensure that the student meets with success. Achievement is necessary for success and for positive self-esteem. To ensure that the child with dyslexia achieves, it is important to ensure that the task is set at the right level – expectations are important, but unrealistic expectations can be dangerous!

School ethos checklist

Here is a school ethos checklist that can be used across the whole school. As indicated earlier, social and emotional factors are the concern of the whole school. Each teacher in each classroom can certainly do their part, but it is always more effective if it is a top-down policy and it has the full support of the school management.

✓ Have we considered individual learning styles?

✓ Do we cater for thinking skills in the curriculum?

✓ How do we fare with moral and spiritual education?

✓ Do we promote school groups, lunchtime groups and after-school groups? Can we do more to promote these?

✓ How do we raise the self-esteem of the students? Can we do more to achieve this?

✓ How do we cater for students who are experiencing emotional difficulties?

✓ How do we achieve student motivation at school level, classroom level and at home?

✓ Have we considered the importance of music and exercise for learning?

✓ Is there music in the classrooms, corridor and recreation areas?

✓ Is there free space dedicated to parents and students for their own purposes?

✓ Is the entrance to the school visually appealing?

✓ Is there a whole-school policy on emotional literacy?

✓ Is there a team spirit among the students – do they have an identity? How is this achieved?

✓ How are the emotional and social needs of the staff catered for at school?

✓ Do staff have open access to management or at least know when management are available?

✓ Is there evidence in the corridors, school handbook, wall displays and in the classrooms that the school is culture-friendly and recognises diversity?

✓ Do the staff have some influence over school policies and practices?

✓ Do the school management have a visible presence for students?

✓ Does the school recognise student success? How is this done?

✓ Do parents feel a sense of ownership within the school? How are they made to feel part of the school?

Motivating children with reading and writing difficulties

In most cases children in nursery and early years need little motivation. Usually they are very much self-motivated. If this is not the case then this in itself will be a warning sign that all is not well. If the child seems reluctant to undertake a task, it is likely that the task is beyond what he or she believes it is. It is important therefore to ensure that the activity and expectations are at the right level for that individual child (Elbeheri, Reid and Everatt 2017). There are different types of motivation (Reid 2007): by task, reward, social motivation, feedback and achievement. These are all relevant to the early years context and are discussed in more detail below.

Motivation by task

For some children the sight, or indeed the thought, of certain types of tasks can be sufficient to de-motivate them, so there is an onus on the teacher to develop achievable tasks. This can be the first major barrier that has to be overcome in order to maintain motivation. Some young children, even if they have only experienced failure once, can become de-motivated and will not want to engage in that activity again. Success is important to prevent de-motivation, and in order to ensure success the task must be achievable – this is where the knowledge and experience of the teacher comes in, to know what the child can or cannot do, how far to push the child and what type of support he or she will need. Great care must therefore be taken when developing tasks to ensure that the tasks are motivating and, importantly, that the child believes the task is achievable. For children with dyslexia it is important that the task is broken down into small steps and that every step represents an achievable and rewarding outcome for the child.

Motivation by reward

Although rewards are useful they should be seen as a short-term strategy – a step towards self-motivation. Rewards are normally only successful in the short term and can help children who need a boost, particularly if they are finding the task challenging. Rewards must also be *achievable* and the learner must *value* the reward. Ideally it is best if the reward is negotiated with the child.

Social motivation and peer group influence

It has already been indicated earlier in this chapter that some children prefer to learn on their own while others need social interaction in order to complete a task. Social interaction can be beneficial as it can help develop important social skills, such as turn-taking and sharing and listening to other people's opinions. The process of helping and working with others can in itself be motivating and is a good model for young children to learn and develop. Group dynamics can, of course, be positive or negative, and it is important to ensure that the composition of the working group is beneficial to all. A constructive and positive group working harmoniously can be a significant motivator. A motivated group will be able to achieve a great deal, and likely more than any one individual can achieve.

Motivation by feedback

Everyone needs feedback to ensure they are on the correct path, but feedback is often used as a means of correcting and grading. Using feedback in this way, the teacher runs the risk of de-motivating the child. It is important that feedback is seen as different from correcting work. Feedback should be continuous and formative and not necessarily come at the end of a task. Moreover, it should be positive or framed in a positive manner. 'Assess, Plan, Do, Review' can provide ongoing feedback and, very importantly, it can lead to a re-assessment and re-development of the task.

Motivation by achievement

The key point here is what we mean by achievement. Achievement is not necessarily reaching the goal set by the teacher or the curriculum objectives. It depends on the child – the learner – and his or her readiness for the task. If a child does not achieve, then the task will need to be revised until he or she can achieve it! This is why the steps used in breaking down tasks are important. But motivation by achievement can be a very important factor in motivation and can help to eradicate any previous failures.

Strategies to develop motivation

Encourage diversity in learning

Young children are still experimenting with learning – some may not even have achieved hand dominance. So it is important to be flexible and not too prescriptive. Encourage diversity in young children's learning preferences. This can be done by offering them choices and giving them the opportunity to utilise their own learning preferences when engaged in activities.

Some factors may restrict this diversity and it is important to reflect on these and ensure that flexibility is used to encourage diversity. These factors include the child's home culture, the school climate and norms, teacher and parent expectations, teaching style and the classroom environment.

Encourage creativity

It is interesting to reflect on the fact that many creative people only take control of their own learning after they leave school. Many fail at school, or may certainly not shine. This is the case with many successful people with dyslexia (Reid 2016b). This is likely due in part to the examination system that often stifles creativity. So it is important that this stifling does not start in the early years. In fact, this is when creativity should be encouraged, as there is usually a bit more leeway in terms of curriculum objectives at this stage. The nature of some of the activities in the nursery – construction, role-play, drama, work in the sand tray, modelling and making items – these are all conducive to developing creativity.

Ensure success with small achievable steps

This point has been made earlier, but it is important to reiterate this here. Success is an essential factor for motivation and, indeed, for eventual independent learning. It is the teacher's responsibility to ensure that the child meets with success. If success is not evident, the task has to be further differentiated. The key point is to ensure that each of the steps is achievable, and to ascertain that knowledge of the child's individual learning preferences and previous learning is available.

Children need to believe in their own abilities

Self-confidence is crucial for success and to maintain motivation. It is important to recognise and acknowledge any achievements, no matter how small they may seem to others or to the child him or herself. Even those who seem to have achieved a great deal of success – in class or in sport – still need and rely on positive feedback to ensure that they can believe in their own abilities. It is often those who seem to have achieved a great deal who have a surprisingly low level of self-belief. This can be because they are not receiving the positive feedback they actually need. The common perception might be that these children do not need it because they know they are successful. The key point here is not to take this for granted and not to assume that successful learners do not need positive and continuous feedback. This is very much the case with those children identified with dyslexia. They, more than anyone, will need positive feedback – even when they are successful.

Use observation

Before developing materials for the class it is important that some knowledge of the individual children within the class is acquired. One of the most effective ways of doing this is through informal observation. The headings below can be used to acquire information on each child. For each of the headings, ask how the child deals with each category (referred to earlier in Chapter 2). For example, how does the child organise information? In what type of learning situations does the child attend best? How does the child interact with others in the class – is it a positive interaction? What type of factors motivate the child to learn? The headings can be used flexibly to obtain any type of information that can be useful, creating a picture of the environmental and learning preferences of the individual:

- organisation
- attention
- sequencing
- interaction
- self-concept
- learning preferences
- motivation/initiative
- independent learning.

Use a range of learning styles in class lessons and activities

One of the signs of a well-prepared classroom lesson or activity is the extent that it deals with a range of learning styles. Each lesson must have auditory, visual, tactile and kinaesthetic elements throughout. This is important to ensure that each child's learning style is accommodated in some way.

Ensure that activities are meaningful

This may seem obvious, but it is a common mistake to assume the child has the basic level of understanding to get maximum benefit from the lesson or the activity. It is important to check on the child's level of understanding and knowledge of the key concepts involved in the lesson. Only if the child has those levels of concepts will the lesson be meaningful.

Minimise pressure

Some children do need some pressure to be motivated, such as competition and rewards, although this should be used carefully – too much pressure can result in total de-motivation as the child may not see the goal as achievable.

Work in groups

Working in groups for children with dyslexia can be a great motivator but at the same time it is important to ensure that the dynamics of the group provide a positive experience for all. It is too easy for one or several children to be 'passengers' and feel 'left out' of a group. Even in groups it might be an idea to pair children who get on well with each other. Group work should also be closely monitored and the group should report on their progress after short intervals.

Use self-assessment

It is never too early to use self-assessment. For very young children this can be in the form of smiley faces, etc. Self-assessment as a learning tool has an important function because it helps children take control of their own learning. They should be encouraged to assess their own progress, and this can be a motivator in itself. The key point is that they should be able to decide what they want to achieve and the teacher's role in this is to guide and monitor their progress.

Self-assessment eventually encourages self-reflection and this helps to develop higher order thinking skills.

Show progression

It is important that the child is able to recognise that he or she is progressing. A framework or even a checklist can help the child note his or her progression. For very young children this can be done with smiley faces.

Concluding thoughts

- Motivation is a key factor in successful learning, and this also applies to very young children.

- Great care must be taken when developing tasks to ensure that they are motivating and, importantly, that the child believes the task is achievable.

- A constructive and positive group working together can be a significant motivator for all children, and can be particularly beneficial to young children with a high risk of dyslexia.

- Feedback should be continuous, positive and formative.

- Acknowledge the young child's learning preferences and encourage diversity in learning. These factors can promote motivation.

- Encourage the child to take responsibility when engaged in a task. This can give him or her a sense of ownership over the task and this in itself is a great motivator.

- Be on the lookout for signs of stress and anxiety and act on this as early as possible.

- It is also important to take the learning environment into account, and to ensure that it is motivating and that there is no or little anxiety that may occur.

Chapter 7

Memory and Information Processing

Dyslexia is essentially a difficulty with information processing. This includes memory and the memory systems that are important for dyslexia are working, short-term and long-term memory. All are important, but difficulty in working memory is often used as an important factor in the diagnosis of dyslexia (Reid and Guise 2017).

Working memory

Working memory involves holding two or more pieces of information at the same time while undergoing a processing activity. A good example of this in the test situation involves saying three or four numbers to a child and the child then has to say them backwards. This is a good test of working memory and is often one that is challenging for children with dyslexia. Guise and Reid (2016) presented a series of workshops on working memory, and responded to the following questions:

- Why is working memory so important?

- How can we test working memory?

- What does low working memory look like?

- How can we support children with working memory problems in class?

- How can we develop and improve memory skills in general?

- How can we promote independent learning and metacognitive awareness in young people with dyslexia?

Guise makes the following key points in relation to these questions, and suggests that working memory is:

- closely linked to learning
- vital in multitasking
- predictive of academic success
- associated with a number of cognitive development disorders.

The characteristics to look out for, according to Guise, are:

- incomplete recall
- difficulties in following every step of instructions
- abandoning a task before it is complete
- problems in retaining *and* processing information
- place-keeping difficulties
- appearing easily distracted/inattentive
- avoiding work that involves concentration
- being forgetful.

It is therefore important to reduce processing demands and to restructure large tasks into separate steps. Computer apps can help a great deal with working memory issues.

Barbra Pavey (2016) reports in some detail on the difference between the various types of memory, and highlights very clearly that the links between dyslexia and memory have been prevalent for some time. She also reports on the work of Alloway (Alloway 2011; Alloway, Seed and Tewolde 2016) who agrees that there is a link between working memory and specific learning difficulties, but also asserts that that while working memory might be a core characteristic of dyslexia, it is not a cause. Pavey (2016) describes the distinction between declarative learning – what the learner knows and how they can display that knowledge – and procedural learning – the actual process of learning such as timing, processing speed and cognitive skills that impact on learning. Much of this is controlled by the central executive part of the brain.

Everatt and Reid (2009) cite the innovative work of Fawcett and Nicolson (2008) on procedural learning. According to Fawcett and Nicolson (2008) there is now extensive evidence that the cerebellum is a brain structure particularly susceptible to insult in the case of premature birth, and that such insults can subsequently lead to a range of motor, language and cognitive problems. Fawcett and Nicolson argue that the cerebellum deficit hypothesis may provide close to a single coherent explanation of the three factors usually associated with dyslexia: reading, writing and spelling. They argue that this can place dyslexia research within a meaningful context in terms of the cognitive neuroscience of learning while maintaining its position as a key educational issue. They also suggest that the cerebellum deficit hypothesis provides an explanation for the overlapping factors between dyslexia and other developmental disorders (see Chapter 8). They argue that one of the hypothesised functions of the cerebellum is in the precise timing of procedures (e.g., several motor movements) that accomplish some sort of behavioural response or task performance. This timing of sequences may play a critical role in making task accomplishment or behavioural skills automatic. They argue that skills need to be automatised before it can be said that they have been learned. Often children with dyslexia display inconsistent performances in carrying out a skill because they have not achieved automaticity. They suggest that reading is subject to automaticity, and since all dyslexia hypotheses predict poor reading as a factor in dyslexia, the automatisation deficit hypothesis would be valid in relation to dyslexia. Their views have clear implications for teaching and learning in that there will be a significant need for over-learning to be utilised with children with dyslexia in the classroom or, indeed, when undertaking any activity.

It is important that there is scope for repetition and repeated practice both at nursery and in the early years. Repetition does not mean that the child is not paying attention or that he or she has forgotten how to do something; it is just that the different components of the learning process take longer to synchronise and consolidate the information and the processes involved in the task. They often have to learn one aspect of the task to the point of mastery, and then tackle another aspect. This will take time and it is important that time is permitted for this.

Organisation is key

Organisation can be the key to an effective memory. Memory has limited capacity, so it important to use strategies to make retention more effective and more complete. Children need to develop effective organisational strategies to ensure that when they are learning new information, it will be understood and retained. The development of effective memory skills has implications for how children remember where equipment is kept and how to carry out a task that they have been shown. Children with dyslexia need to practise a great deal before tasks and information can be accessed automatically. They therefore need a great deal of repetition.

Strategies to help memory

It is important that realistic strategies are provided, and these can be implemented as part of the teaching process without the child being aware that it is a memory strategy that is being practised. Some examples are shown below.

Prioritise

Children with dyslexia can only do one task at a time. Everyone, including young children, always has too many things to do and too many things to remember. It is interesting to ponder on the following view. Although people's brain cells diminish as they get older, memory skills can actually improve (up to a certain age!). This is because maturity, strategies and experience of learning all help with retention and recall of information.

Young children in the nursery or at school are surrounded by a great deal of information and stimuli, and it may be necessary for the teacher to help the child by highlighting the key things in the room or when remembering information. It is necessary therefore to *prioritise*, but for some children this can be difficult and so it is necessary to practise. When a young child has a list of things to do, he or she can become confused and it can become difficult for him or her to decide what to do first and what is less important. This can apply to daily tasks as well as to specific areas of learning.

Prioritising actions helps clear the mind of competing tasks to be carried out, and this will allow the child to focus exclusively on the task in hand and not to worry about the other things that have to be carried out.

Plan

One of the benefits of prioritising when undertaking an activity is that it can help with both a sequence as well as planning for the various steps in the activity. This helps to unburden the load on the memory and can make the task less formidable.

Monitor

This is important, as through monitoring the teacher can reassure the child that he or she is on the right track.

Praise and reinforce

Praise can be used to reinforce learning. It is therefore important to build in constructive feedback into every learning activity the child is engaged in, and this should, of course, highlight the positive aspects or be framed in positive language. This can be done by first stating what the child has achieved and then going on to discuss how this can be improved, which can be done in the form of a suggestion.

Organise

One of the reasons why some people have a good memory is because they are able to organise the information at the time of learning and immediately afterwards. It is important therefore that the child receives assistance to help him or her organise the information as he or she is learning.

Sequence and order

This is an important factor for memory work – some people can remember information better if it is sequenced for them. This can be done in history through the use of a timeline to sequence events, and can also be done when studying a novel, for example. Many children need this type of structure and it is a good way of chunking events together. For example, a task to practice this could be to chunk all the events that happen in the first chapter of a book or in the reign of a monarch in history and to make a list of these. The child can then illustrate these to make it more meaningful.

Some memory tips

- *Chunking:* This involves putting like items together, which eases the burden on the memory.

- *Organise information:* This also involves putting similar items together and getting rid of superfluous information.

- *Take time:* Children with dyslexia will take longer to take the information in and to retain it for future use. They will need a lot of repetition, over-learning and practise, which will take time.

- *Repeat and reinforce:* This follows on from the above. Teachers need to be ready to use a range of multisensory strategies in order to repeat the task using as many modalities as possible. This in itself is a good way of reinforcing. Discussing and articulating what they are learning is also a good way of reinforcing for children with dyslexia.

KEY POINT

When repeating information, make sure you do this in a range of different ways. Use memory cards, visuals, headings, summaries, notes and discussion. All these can be repeating the same information, but use various means to do this. This is how information is consolidated and mastered. Mastery is the aim of learning, and this will take time and considerable over-learning for children with dyslexia.

- *Make a plan of the steps involved in the activity (small steps):* This is very important for children with dyslexia as small steps can be huge steps for them. The steps should be made as small as possible until they can do the activity. This is essentially differentiation.

- *Use multisensory strategies:* It is more effective to use all your senses when learning.

- *Make connections:* You need to make connections all the time when learning. This makes learning meaningful and it can aid understanding and the development of concepts. The main connection is between previous learning and new learning. Questions the child needs to consider are: Is there anything about the new learning that is familiar? What is familiar and why? This will help children connect between the previous and new learning and make learning more efficient.

- *Imagine:* It is well known that young children can have very vivid imaginations. The point about this is that it is their own construction, and therefore they are more likely to remember the detail – they can use their imaginative skills to remember new information they are learning. They can integrate the new material into one of their imaginative stories. Encouraging the use of imagination can also help with creativity and thinking skills.

- *Drama:* Learning should be active – this means the child must be fully involved in the learning activity. The more active the learner is, the more likely the information will be understood and retained. This activity could be in the form of drama. Drama is excellent for developing children's speech and for many other areas of learning. It is also fun. Cecchini (no date), in an article in *Earlychildhood NEWS*, indicated that dramatic play can promote social and emotional development – it can help children develop empathy, to control impulses, and also helps them with sharing ideas and problem-solving as well as developing language skills.

- *Understanding:* This is vitally important for effective learning and for memory. It is important to take time to ensure that the information is fully understood by the child. If not, it is unlikely it will be remembered.

KEY POINT

Understanding is the key to the efficient use of memory. Understanding comes before retention but will make retention easier, particularly over the long term.

- *Talk:* For some children talking about it is the only way in which they can retain and understand information. This can make the information meaningful for them, and some children need to articulate what they are doing. This is good practice and should be encouraged. It is particularly useful for learners with dyslexia as it helps with the thinking aloud process, which can eventually lead to what is known as metacognition, being aware of how you think and how you tackle a problem.

In summary, children with dyslexia usually have working memory deficits. It is argued that this is because they have a restricted number of strategies available to them to keep information in working memory long enough to process that information – often it is lost before it is processed. This means they will have little chance of retaining that information and the information will not be transferred to long-term memory.

Gathercole and Alloway (2008) indicate that working memory is seen as having a vital role in holding information in short-term memory long enough to act on it, and in both the storage and retrieval of information from long-term memory. They also argue that the role of short-term working memory in dyslexia is not always given the attention it deserves, and the relevance of memory to learning can, in fact, be overlooked in the planning of intervention programmes for children with dyslexia.

Guidance for Identifying and Supporting Young Children with Special Educational Needs for Early Years Settings, Schools and Support Services (Sure Start Children's Centres 2010) indicates that by 4 years of age children should be able to remember details from a story read to them, and most children can. Children with dyslexia, however, many not remember the details but may get the general gist of the storyline. They may also have a difficulty with the sequence of the story.

Information processing

Information processing is very much connected to memory. All the memory processes are part of what we call information processing. To fully understand how young children learn and how this relates to dyslexia it is necessary to understand the information processing cycle. This is important because, essentially, dyslexia is a difficulty with information processing, and children with dyslexia can have difficulties at a number of stages of the information processing cycle.

There are three key areas involved in dyslexia and all are integral to the information processing cycle. These are the planning of the learning activity, the actual presentation of lessons and activities and the nature and extent of the differentiation carried out, including the accessibility of the materials. There is a tendency to focus on the materials/resources, and this suggests that with the right resources and materials dyslexic children will be able to learn effectively. But this does not mean they will be able to process the information effectively. Certainly obtaining appropriate resources is vital, but this does not preclude the need for the teacher to embark on lesson planning and differentiation as a means of meeting the needs of young children with dyslexia.

It is perhaps more helpful to view the difficulties experienced by dyslexic children as barriers to learning. It follows that if these barriers can be identified through examining the curriculum and the tasks presented to the child, this will go a long way towards meeting these needs. Expectations are also important, and realigning expectations is part of the differentiation process. This means that although the child may have differences or difficulties in the processing of information, intervention needs to encompass a wider angle and not just focus on the child's deficits or difficulties. The task, curriculum, presentation and duration of the task, as well as curriculum expectations, are all important.

Cognition

Cognition is important for learning. This describes the actual processes involved in learning a piece of information, which relates to memory, understanding, organising and generally making sense of information and retaining it for future use. Often children with dyslexia have cognitive difficulties and this relates to difficulties with memory. This also includes organising information as well as memory, and can represent quite serious difficulties that the dyslexic child needs to overcome in order to become an effective and independent learner.

What is important, however, is that good teaching can help to overcome all of these cognitive difficulties. Much can be done to aid the child's memory, and assistance by the teacher to help the dyslexic child organise information can help him or her learn more effectively. The teacher can therefore play a key role in helping dyslexic children overcome cognitive difficulties.

Metacognition

Cognition, as indicated earlier in this chapter, means learning; metacognition means learning to learn. This implies that children can be taught to be more effective learners. Flavell (1979) greatly influenced the field of metacognition and its applications to the classroom, and metacognition has now been given considerable prominence in schools and in assessment and curriculum activities.

This is very important for children with dyslexia. The research indicates that children with dyslexia may be weak in metacognitive awareness and therefore have difficulty in knowing how to go about tackling a problem – for example, they may not be sure on *how* to interpret a question or to work out the most efficient way of answering it, or, in fact, to remember any piece of information.

Wray (1994) suggests that teachers should teach metacognitive strategies directly and always within the context of meaningful experiences. This can be included in children's project work. Metacognition, he argues, should be an integral part of the learning process, and to be an effective component it should be embedded within the curriculum and within curricular activities.

The development of metacognitive skills can be aided by programmes that are essentially 'study skills' programmes, and these can be tailored for young children. There is a kind of myth that study skills are really for students further up school, but I have always indicated that study skills should start as young as possible. Very often they are seen as part of examination preparation, but this is too late. Becoming efficient in studying and learning helps the child make connections between different pieces of information, and this can help with the transfer of learning and generally more efficient use of information.

Zone of Proximal Development (ZPD)

The ZPD refers to the interaction between the teacher and the child, how much of the new learning can be independently accessed by the child, and how much the teacher is required to mediate in order for the child to access full understanding and develop further related concepts. This is of vital importance to the nursery and early years setting. The idea is to promote independence in learning so that the child can do the task him or herself unaided, but to begin with, the child will need assistance, or scaffolding (see below). For example, in learning to swim the scaffold could be the instructor's supporting hand or 'water wings'. To gain independence these items have to be removed. But if they are removed too soon, before the skill has been learned, the child may fail and experience 'learned helplessness'. This means that the experience of failure has such an impact that the child is reluctant to try again. ZPD refers to the point when the child is ready for the scaffolds to be removed. If they are not removed when the child is ready, this might restrict progression as the child will be receiving support when it is not necessary. It is a tricky situation but one that is relevant to the early years and certainly one that is relevant to dyslexia. Children with dyslexia do need support, but over-supporting them will be doing them no favours! Burden (2002) suggests that when there are signs that independent cognitive activity is taking place, the scaffolds should gradually be removed at appropriate moments.

Scaffolding

Scaffolding is essentially a process by which a teacher provides children with a temporary framework for learning. If this is carried out appropriately, the structure that is provided will encourage children to develop their own ideas, and promote the use of initiative, motivation and resourcefulness. The idea is that eventually, the initial scaffolding is removed altogether when the children no longer need it.

Study skills

Well-developed study skills habits in the early years can provide a sound foundation for tackling new material further up the school. Many children are able to learn new material intuitively without too much bother. Children with dyslexia, however, often have to make more of an effort and consciously use memory and other learning strategies.

A principal factor in a study skills programme that could be considered in the early years includes *sequencing information*. Children with dyslexia may have some difficulty in retelling a story or providing information in the correct sequence, so it is important that the correct sequencing of information is encouraged, and exercises that help to do this can be used. For example, in recounting the events in a story, a framework might include:

- How did the story start?

- What happened after that?

- What was the main part?

- How did it end?

A framework could be provided for recalling the story, and this can include aspects such as:

- Background: Where is the story set?

- Context: What was the weather like and how do you imagine the background conditions – hills, towns, countryside, etc.?

- Characters: Who are they and what are they like?

- Beginning of the story: Was it a good beginning – why?

- Main part: How did you know this was the main part?

- Events: What took place during the story?

- Conclusion: How did it end? Was it a good ending and was it what you were expecting?

A study skills programme should also include the use of visual skills that can help the child visualise or imagine details that may be inferred in the passage but not explicitly shown. This can lead to inferential reading and is extremely important for children with dyslexia, because they are often pre-occupied with reading for accuracy and may just get some meaning, but seldom get to the inferring stage where they have to read between the lines. It is good to practice this as young as possible, and it can certainly be used in the early years classroom.

Wray (2009) suggests the following framework can be useful:

- Activating prior knowledge (What do I know?).

- What do I want to know?

- What did I learn?

He argues that there is a great deal of research that indicates the importance of children's prior knowledge in their understanding of new knowledge (see, for example, Keene and Zimmerman 2007). He also argues that prior knowledge needs to be brought to the forefront of the child's mind and made explicit, if it is to be useful.

The framework below, based on the KWL (Know, Want to know, Learn) grid, is a good example. It was developed as a teaching strategy in the US and is a simple but effective strategy that takes children through the steps of the research process and also records their learning. It gives children a logical structure for tackling tasks in many areas of the curriculum and it is this combination of a simple but logical support scaffolding that seems to be so useful to children with dyslexia.

A KWL grid

What do I KNOW about this already?	What do I WANT to know?	What did I LEARN?

Mind mapping

Tony Buzan has some wonderful materials on mind mapping such as *Mind Maps for Kids* (2005). Mind mapping can be an excellent strategy even with young children because it uses visual skills and can also provide opportunities for lateral thinking and creativity.

Concluding thoughts

Although children are usually well into primary school before they become more adept at using memory strategies, it is never too young to start training them to use memory strategies. Sometimes we do it without thinking, but it is a good idea to encourage children to think of good ways to remember important information. Some reading programmes, such as Letterland (Letterland International Ltd 1997), use pictograms in addition to friezes, code cards, flashcards, word books, cassettes and songbooks, copymasters, workbooks, games and resources and software to help children remember individual letters and words. Wendon (1993), who created the Letterland programme, suggests that we should take our lead from the children and ask them how they prefer to remember or do a certain task. This will help them to remember the information more effectively.

This, in my opinion, is sound advice as it is important to encourage children – including very young children – to become independent learners. The learning experience is crucial, and equally it is important that children are aware of how they tackled a task and how they can use the same techniques and strategies the next time round. This can also instil them with confidence that they can remember how to do certain things and can become very proficient in this.

Working in groups may also be useful, as the children can help each other to remember items. Group games may be useful, as they use multisensory strategies, and using all the modalities is essential for developing effective memory skills.

Chapter 8

Specific Learning Difficulties

The term 'specific learning difficulties', or SpLD, is in common use internationally. It incorporates a broad range of difficulties and these difficulties can overlap. The labels usually associated with SpLD include: dyslexia, dyspraxia, dyscalculia, dysgraphia and attention-deficit hyperactivity disorder (ADHD).

The term 'SpLD' is useful because, as mentioned above, there is often an overlap between the various difficulties, and there can be any combination of overlap – for example, dyslexia and dyspraxia, dyspraxia and attention difficulties (including ADHD). This overlap is often called 'comorbidity' or 'co-existence' and there is a growing body of evidence to suggest that comorbidity may, in fact, be highly prevalent (see, for example, Bishop and Snowling 2004). This is not new factor and this type of overlap has been noted for many years now. Biedermanet *et al.* (1990) showed how research evidence indicated that more than 50 per cent of children with a diagnosis of developmental coordination disorder (DCD) (dyspraxia) meet the requirements of at least two disorders. Ramus, Pidgeon and Frith (2003) suggested that many children with dyslexia show an overlap with ADHD and dyspraxia, and Kaplan *et al.* (1998) reported that 63 per cent of the sample they studied also had dyspraxia.

The broad range of difficulties associated with SpLD can be subdivided into the following, and can be noted in the early years in some form:

- language-related (including reading, spelling and writing)

- attention

- motor

- social

- mathematical.

Overlap, continuum and intervention

So what do we mean by the term 'SpLD'? A frequently asked question is what is the difference between SpLD and dyslexia? SpLD refers to a specific processing difficulty that is significantly discrepant in relation to that individual's other processing abilities. Some of these discrepancies can provide a profile with a label such as dyspraxia, dysgraphia or dyscalculia. It is essentially an 'umbrella' term used to describe a number of different conditions. The Special Needs Assessment Profile (SNAP) (see Chapter 3) was developed in order to help teachers separate the different strands that often comprise SpLD, so that they can see precisely what the main problems are and the individual characteristics.

Each of the conditions usually has a number of specific characteristics, which may be found in dyslexia, dyspraxia, dyscalculia and dysgraphia and also attention difficulties, with or without hyperactivity (see the Glossary at the end of the book for further explanation). These conditions are usually referred to as syndromes, and will have a number of characteristic criteria.

It is important to note that there is some controversy and disagreement relating to the factors that constitute individual and discrete syndromes such as those mentioned above. Elliott and Grigorenko (2014a, 2014b) dispute the use of the label 'dyslexia', and argue that we should be focusing on the precise characteristics of reading difficulties and not differentiating the different types of reading difficulties by referring to the 'dyslexia' label. They therefore call for an end to the use of the 'dyslexia' label and for it to be replaced by more detailed descriptors of specific literacy skills and deficits underpinning reading difficulty. They argue that the term 'dyslexia' is little more than an artificial construct and conceptually problematic, although they agree with McDonald (2009) that it can help in gaining access to additional resources or support.

Not surprisingly, these views resulted in a surge of responses arguing against Elliott and Grigorenko's position (see, for example, BDA 2015; Nicolson 2005, 2016). Nicolson (2016) argues that we can characterise differences between dyslexic and poor readers, while Elliott and Grigorenko argue that this is not the case. Like the BDA position (see below), Nicolson also believes that a diagnosis of dyslexia can be useful to the child and the family. Unlike Elliott, Nicolson's conceptual framework for dyslexia is a broad one incorporating a range of constructs including learning differences (which skills and knowledge appear to be weak), executive functioning (how adequate their capabilities are), affective state (the existence of school phobias, disaffection and what triggers these) and the interactions between learning abilities and teaching methods (including strengths – what the child is good at and what they enjoy doing as well as the learning environment and teaching procedures). Nicolson argues that the way ahead is to promote higher quality expert assessment for dyslexia rather than 'assessment' of dyslexia!

The BDA position statement indicates that dyslexia is a well-established and well-researched disorder. The BDA (2015) comments that it is in touch with many thousands of teachers and parents, and able to gather first-hand accounts of how dyslexia impacts the individual pupil, the adults and the family. They maintain that the current academic debate serves no useful purpose, and in many ways it is insulting to those who experience dyslexia and to their families as well as the many thousands of teachers, including those funded under the government *Rose Review* recommendations (2009). These teachers, they commented, have worked extremely hard to complete accredited courses in dyslexia. The BDA accredits courses in dyslexia through the Accreditation Board, and highlights that the majority of these courses are validated at university level. In short, the BDA believes that both the research basis and practical impact of dyslexia is widely recognised, and there is no fresh or convincing evidence to counter this.

Elliot and Grigorenko's position can be very confusing for teachers and parents and, in fact, can call into question the use, and perhaps the misuse, of labels. This means that we have to be careful when applying labels to individual children.

Children with SpLD will therefore display a specific difficulty in one or more of the cognitive processes relating to learning (Singleton 2002). An important point to note is that each of these syndromes can be seen within a spectrum of difficulties – a continuum – and the degree and extent of the characteristics can vary between individual children, which makes identification and assessment quite challenging, more so because there can also be an overlap between the features of the different syndromes.

To aid the process of making sense of the characteristics of SpLD, Weedon and Reid (2004, 2008) and Weedon, Reid and Ruttle (2017) (see Chapter 3) developed a SNAP, which looks a number of the presenting characteristics that make up learning difficulties. Using a dedicated matrix it is possible to identify the cluster of difficulties presented by different children (see below).

A child with dyslexia may therefore also have attention difficulties and dyspraxic difficulties. It can also be stated at this point that some of the characteristics of dyslexia, such as phonological difficulties, working memory difficulties and processing speed are often found in children with other needs (see the Glossary at the end of the book). Dyslexia is, however, the most prevalent of the conditions that make up SpLD. Additionally, literacy has a major part to play in accessing the curriculum, and difficulties with literacy will restrict curricular access for all children, irrespective of the label.

Characteristics and common concerns

It can be suggested that the label is only the starting point, and that attention needs to be paid to the specific characteristics of the child's profile. It is therefore possible to identify what might be called a 'core of common concerns', which would imply that we could focus on 'common' areas of difficulties when developing tasks and activities as well as teaching programmes. For example, some common concerns that can be developed and included in planning for learning may be social skills, working memory difficulties, recording information through writing and processing speed. These areas can be tackled in a group situation, but the individual needs of the children in the class, whether dyslexic, dyspraxic, dyscalculic or ADHD, will still be met using this type of approach.

The table below can be used to show how children with different syndromes or difficulties may have overlapping concerns. (Make notes or ticks for each of the concerns and each of the categories.)

Areas of concern

Concern	Dyslexia	Dyspraxia	Dyscalculia	Dysgraphia	ADHD
Keeping on task					
Memory					
Literacy skills					
Organisation					
Social skills					
Self-esteem					
Processing speed					

Overlapping syndromes

Some of SpLD that have relevance for the nursery and early years classrooms and that can overlap with dyslexia are now described.

Dyspraxia/developmental coordination disorder (DCD)

Dyspraxia and DCD are motor/coordination difficulties. These can be seen within a continuum from mild to severe, and can impact on fine motor activities such as pencil grip and scissors control and gross motor activities such as movement and balance. Portwood (2001) describes dyspraxia as motor difficulties caused by perceptual problems, especially visual-motor and kinaesthetic motor difficulties.

The *Diagnostic and Statistical Manual of Mental Disorders* (5th edn) (DSM-V) criteria for DCD (APA 2013) indicates that dyspraxia/DCD relates to motor performance that is substantially below expected levels, given the person's chronological age and previous opportunities for skill acquisition. The poor motor performance may manifest as coordination problems, poor balance, clumsiness, dropping or bumping into things, marked delays in achieving developmental motor milestones (e.g., walking, crawling, sitting) or in the acquisition of basic motor skills (e.g., catching, throwing, kicking, running, jumping, hopping, cutting, colouring, printing, writing). It also indicates that this impairment must significantly interfere with academic achievement or activities of daily life, and that the onset of symptoms should be evident in the early developmental period.

These children may, however, have a range of other difficulties that can be associated with other types of SpLD. It may therefore be more useful for the teacher to be aware of the specific characteristics of an individual child's profile. This also highlights the view that children can have different profiles for the same difficulty. For example, some children with characteristics of DCD may also have significant difficulties in working memory, while other children may not. Characteristics, as opposed to labels, can take on a more descriptive role. Characteristics for a number of SpLD can include, to a greater or lesser extent, aspects relating to:

- working memory deficits
- auditory processing
- fine motor difficulties
- phonological difficulties
- non-verbal difficulties
- literacy difficulties.

These processing difficulties will affect attention, memory and reading. It is not surprising therefore that some overlap exists between them. One of the common elements shared with all SpLD is the low level of self-esteem. This can be addressed without recourse to a label as a self-esteem programme can have a beneficial effect on all children. Jones (2005) suggests that even low-level intervention significantly increases self-esteem and has the additional effect of improving classroom performance. This point is reinforced by Kirby (2003, 2006) who suggests that it is important that the child with DCD obtains support and practice in building relationships and coping at all stages of schooling. Macintyre (2001) and Macintyre and McVitty (2004) emphasise the early years stage, and indicate quite strongly that this is the key time for identification and intervention, and many of the activities they recommend, such as hopping and skipping, are ideal for early years.

Children with dyslexia in the early years can have difficulty with basic coordination tasks such as dressing and changing for activities such as PE. Strategies that can minimise the impact of this include using loose clothes and even loose socks, and elastic waistbands to avoid difficult fasteners (Velcro fasteners are very useful).

There are also many games that can help with DCD/dyspraxia. These include hand/eye coordination games such as juggling balls, basketball net practice, table tennis and magnetic games, such as a pool-like fun fishing or even maze games.[1] Others include memory games and board games as well as puzzles and even jigsaw puzzles, as these are good for hand/eye coordination.

Attention deficit disorders (ADHD)

The criteria for diagnosis of ADHD (APA 2013) indicate factors relating to inattentiveness, hyperactivity and impulsivity. The criteria indicated, which include aspects such as 'often has difficulty in sustaining attention in tasks or play activities', 'often runs about or climbs excessively' and 'often interrupts or intrudes on others', needs to have persisted for at least six months to a degree that is maladaptive and inconsistent with developmental level. Although there has been considerable amount of literature on ADHD, there is still controversy regarding the unitary model of ADHD as a discrete syndrome. There is also some debate on the nature of the syndrome and particularly its primary causes and intervention (Reid 2006). It is useful to place the symptoms and characteristics of ADHD into a framework to help highlight the different strands and various characteristics that can contribute to ADHD.

Framework for attention difficulties

At the *neurological level* the following factors may be relevant:

- Hemispheric preferences – usually a child with ADHD would be a right hemisphere processor.

---

1   See www.crossboweducation.co.uk

- Saliency determination – recognising what is relevant; often a child with ADHD would have difficulty in recognising the relevant features of a conversation or written work.

- Auditory distractibility – this implies that the child is easily distracted by noise of some sort.

- Tactile distractibility – similarly touch could be distracting, and often the child with ADHD may want to touch in order to be distracted.

- Motor inhibition – often children with ADHD may have difficulty in inhibiting a response and may react impulsively in some situations.

In relation to *cognitive dimensions* the following factors may be significant:

- Depth of processing – if the child is not attending to a stimuli, it is likely that the processing will be at a shallow as opposed to deep level. Clearly if this is the case, the child will not gain much from the learning experience, either in understanding or in pleasure – therefore the learning experience will not be automatically reinforced.

- Information processing – just as in the case of dyslexia, the information processing cycle of input, cognition and output can be influential in identifying the type of difficulties that may be experienced by children with attention difficulties. This would therefore have implications for teaching.

- Metacognitive factors – this is important for reinforcing learning, for transferring learning and for developing concepts; it is likely that the child with attention difficulties will have poor metacognitive skills, and this will also make learning less meaningful and have a negative effect on attention span.

In relation to *educational or classroom factors* the following can be considered:

- Factors associated with free flight – this means that the child will have little control over the thinking process, essentially what may be described as a right hemisphere processing style.

This would mean that some structure is required to help direct the child's thinking processes.

- Unpredictability, inconsistency and impulsivity – this again indicates that there is little control over learning, and that many actions would be impulsive.

- Pacing skills and on-task factors – these again indicate a lack of control over learning, and that students with attention difficulties have a problem with pacing the progress of work and therefore may tire easily or finish prematurely.

Attention difficulties can be identified within an education setting – if a child is said to have attention difficulties, these should be obvious in every aspect of school life and in all activities.

ADHD and dyslexia

It is not surprising that there is a strong view that an overlap exists between ADHD and dyslexia. Many of the cognitive attention processing mechanisms that children with ADHD seem to have difficulty with, such as short-term memory, sustained attention, processing speed and accuracy in copying, can also be noted in children with dyslexia.

Willcutt and Pennington (2000) noted in a large-scale study that children with reading difficulties were more likely than children without reading disabilities to meet the criteria for ADHD, and that the association was stronger for inattention than for hyperactivity.

Specific learning difficulties and alternative therapies

One of the areas that may have far-reaching consequences and potential is that of the interventions that can be classed as 'alternative therapies'. These tend to be popular, new and often have media appeal. This is not to say that they are not helpful – in fact, some of the evidence seems to support the use of some of these alternative forms of intervention.

Diet

There has been considerable popular coverage on the use of food additives, and much anecdotal evidence to support the view that these may have an adverse affect on learning, particularly for children with ADHD. Richardson and Puri (2000) suggest that there is a wide spectrum of conditions in which deficiencies of highly unsaturated fatty acids appear to have some influence. Further, Richardson argues that fatty acids can have an extremely important influence on dyslexia, dyspraxia and ADHD. She argues that it is not too controversial to suggest that there is a high incidence of overlap between these three syndromes – in fact, she suggests that an overlap between dyslexia and ADHD can be around 30–50 per cent and even higher in the case of dyspraxia. Richardson argues that the truly essential fatty acids (EFA) that cannot be synthesised by the body must be provided in the diet – these are linoleic acid (omega 6 series) and alpha-linoleic acid (omega 3 series). She suggests that the longer-chain, highly unsaturated fatty acids (HUFA), which the brain needs, can normally be synthesised from EFAs, but this conversion process can be severely affected and limited by dietary and lifestyle factors. Some of the dietary factors that can, for example, block the conversion of EFA to HUFA include excess saturated fats, hydrogenated fats found in processed foods and deficiencies in vitamins and minerals as well as excessive consumption of coffee and alcohol and smoking.

Richardson suggests that the claims connecting hyperactivity and lack of EFA are not new. Studies on dyspraxia have also highlighted the possibility of links with EFA, and suggested that fatty acid supplements can be beneficial (Sordy 1995, 1997). In relation to dyslexia and ADHD, Richardson suggests that fatty acid supplements have also been shown to be successful, and supplementation has been associated with improvements in reading. Richardson also reports on school-based trials indicating that this intervention can be realistically applied in schools (Portwood 2001, 2002; Richardson 2002).

Exercise and movement

There has been a long-standing interest in exercise and therapies based on movement for children with SpLD. Fitts and Posner (1967) provided an account of the learning stages in motor skill development and particularly the development of automaticity. Denckla and Rudel (1976) found that children with dyslexia had a deficit in rapid automatised naming, and suggested that children with dyslexia are characterised by a 'non-specific developmental awkwardness', irrespective of athletic ability. In terms of intervention, Ayres' work (1979) has been developed considerably by Blythe (2001), Blythe and Goddard (2000) and McPhillips, Hepper and Mulhern (2000).[2]

The work of Dennison and Hargrove (1985) and Dennison and Dennison (1989, 2001) in relation to Brain Gym® and Hannaford (1995, 1997) on the importance of dominance and laterality, and particularly the influence of dominance patterns on learning, has also been influential in classrooms, particularly with children with SpLD.

A number of programmes can be used for children with SpLD that involve movement and that claim to have beneficial cognitive and learning effects.

An overlapping spectrum

Despite their separate diagnostic labels, the clinical overlap between dyslexia, dyspraxia, ADHD and the autistic spectrum is high, and 'pure' cases are the exception, not the rule. This means, for example, that around half of the dyslexic population is likely to be dyspraxic and vice versa, and the mutual overlap between ADHD and dyspraxia is also around 50 per cent. Dyslexia and ADHD co-occur in 30–50 per cent of cases, although this association is stronger for inattention than for hyperactivity-impulsivity. All of these conditions also show some overlap with the autistic spectrum, although in severe cases, the autism diagnosis always takes precedence. In summary, criteria for SpLD are as follows:

Dyspraxia, which means difficulties with:

- gross motor skills – balance and coordination
- speech and language
- social skills
- attention/concentration

---

2   See the Institute for Neuro Physiological Psychology at www.inpp.org.uk

- visual/motor skills

- spatial awareness

- laterality

- fine motor tasks.

Dysgraphia, which can mean displaying:

- letter inconsistencies

- mixture of upper and lower case

- irregular letter size and shapes

- unfinished letters

- reluctance to write

- poor visual perception

- poor fine motor skills.

Intervention

Many of the strategies that need to be used to help children with SpLD can be similar even though the label may be different. Hughes and Cooper (2007) provide a good example of this in their book *Understanding and Supporting Children with ADHD*. They suggest the following strategies for children with ADHD:

- Avoid confrontational situations.

- Show the child respect.

- Listen to the child's concerns.

- Avoid distraction.

- Keep instructions to a minimum – one at a time.

- Provide reassurance on tasks.

- Split tasks up into short tasks with breaks.

- Enable the child to complete tasks.

- Scaffold the child's work.

- Provide a routine.

- Provide outlets for active behaviour.

- Provide a clear structure in the class.

The interesting point is that all of these factors can be useful for children with dyspraxia, dyscalculia and dyslexia as well as ADHD.

Concluding thoughts

The term 'specific learning difficulties' on its own may be confusing for the teacher and for the parent. It can, of course, be given a more precise explanation by describing the precise characteristics and the actual syndrome it is closest to, such as dyslexia. But at the same time, we need to remember that the overlap is not the exception but occurs in the majority of children who are diagnosed with one or more of the SpLD. From this point of view, it serves a useful purpose.

It has a similar connotation to the term 'learning disabilities' used in the US and Canada. In DSM-V this is now referred to as a 'specific learning disorder'. The argument is that broadening the diagnostic category reflects the latest scientific understanding of the condition. Specific symptoms, such as difficulty in reading, are just symptoms, and in many cases one symptom points to a larger set of problems.[3]

Once again, the key point – whatever the label used or indeed the presenting difficulties – is early identification coupled with early intervention. This cannot be emphasised strongly enough. Additionally, it is good practice and helpful to obtain the precise characteristics of the child's difficulties and, as indicated earlier in Chapter 3, this can be revealed through thorough testing and insightful observation.

---

3   This fact sheet provides a helpful explanation: www.dsm5.org/Documents/Specific%20Learning%20Disorder%20Fact%20Sheet.pdf

Chapter 9

Issues and Considerations

This book has provided guidance on identification, assessment and intervention in the early years, but it is clear that there is no straightforward and definitive answer – in other words, there is no one way of tackling this, and there is still some controversy over some of the issues. This chapter therefore looks at some of these issues, and also some of the key areas for consideration, such as the role of parents and early screening. Key issues discussed here include EAL and the implications for assessment and intervention, school liaison and the role of parents.

Dyslexia in different languages

Linda Siegel (2016) indicates that dyslexia is primarily a language disorder, involving difficulties with hearing and confusing sounds within words, isolating and manipulating sounds within words, retrieving the pronunciation of letters and groups of letters quickly, problems with verbal working memory, often less developed vocabulary skills and sometimes word-finding difficulties. She also states that it is reasonable to expect that when people with dyslexia are required to learn an additional language, they may very well experience difficulties. She argues that diagnosing the causes of this, that is, whether it is due to inadequate exposure to the language or to some other factors such as dyslexia, is a tricky matter. Since there are no formal tests in many of the first languages – other than English – Siegel argues that it is important to ascertain what language experiences the EAL child has had with peers, and in particular, if the child went to pre-school where many of the children and the teachers were native English speakers.

This type of pre-school experience would provide a rich English language experience, and this should be sufficient for most learners to acquire English. Siegel argues that having older siblings who speak English is also key. She states that if the child plays with native English speakers in the neighbourhood, the EAL child will learn a colloquial English and bring this experience to formal schooling. If reading or pre-reading tests are carried out with the child and the results are within the average range, it is unlikely that the child is dyslexic. She further states that, on the other hand, if the child's performance on reading tasks is low, it is likely that he or she is dyslexic, providing that the child has had sufficient exposure to reading instruction in English. It is therefore important to ascertain the nature of the child's exposure to English, as this is an important determinant of a potential diagnosis of dyslexia, or even the identification of children at risk of dyslexia.

Siegel further argues that there is also the issue of when children at risk of dyslexia are noted, that we then need to ascertain what the most appropriate intervention strategies are. She describes a large-scale study she led in North Vancouver in British Columbia, Canada, in which 30 languages were spoken in addition to English in the geographical area in the study. The most common language was Cantonese.

Siegel suggests that knowing the names of the letters, as in the Wide Range Achievement Test (WRAT), is a good predictor of subsequent reading difficulties, as is the level of the child's phonological awareness. The Comprehensive Test of Phonological Processing (CTOPP) can be used for this. These are good indicators of risk because the child would have been exposed to this and should be familiar enough with letter names and sounds to complete this test at an adequate level. Siegel and colleagues found that 50 per cent of the EAL children had scores on these tasks in the range that would considered to be 'at risk'.

Two phonological programmes were therefore put into operation for these children (and all others in the class) and the responses and progress were analysed. The other programme used was called Reading 44,[1] which is designed to teach reading comprehension and vocabulary skills and is delivered to all children in the classroom. The results indicated that 1.5 per cent of the English L1 group had significant reading problems (dyslexia) and 1.5 per cent of the EAL

---

1   This was called 'Reading 44', as it was developed in school district 44 in North Vancouver, British Columbia.

group had significant reading problems (dyslexia). These results highlight the importance of an appropriate early reading intervention programme. Siegel did indicate that the study showed some positive aspects of bilingualism such as enhanced visual memory skills, which aided spelling.

One of the surprising findings that was very promising in the EAL population related to higher reading comprehension, and Siegel and colleagues commented that this was pleasantly surprising, and indicated that EAL status should not be a barrier to developing reading comprehension. Siegel concluded that children with EAL could be assessed for 'high risk of dyslexia' in the early years of schooling, but that appropriate early intervention could reduce the incidence of reading difficulties. The research team also went further to postulate that in some circumstances being bilingual was actually an advantage for children with dyslexia, as some positive aspects of their first language transferred to their second language.

Role of culture

Bilingualism and multilingualism are areas that can present a challenge to educators, particularly in relation to assessment and teaching. It is widely acknowledged that dyslexia can occur across languages, cultures, SES, race and gender (BPS 1999).

Cultural and language factors in many standardised tests (Everatt, Adams and Smythe 2000) can mitigate against the child whose first language is not English. Many have been developed for use with a monolingual population, and this can account for the under-estimation, or, indeed, the misdiagnosis, of dyslexia in bilingual children. Landon (2001, p.182) addressed this by asking, 'What factors appear to lead to low rates of detection of dyslexia amongst bilingual learners and could the same factors also explain the poor standards of literacy amongst many learners of English as an Additional Language (EAL learners)?' The importance of these questions is that they actually investigate the issues and provide a good example of the types of questions teachers need to ask when assessing children who are bilingual. To answer the questions presented by Landon, the range of factors that contribute to dyslexia must be considered.

Culture-fair assessment can be of two types. It is important to develop assessment materials in the language being taught, but to make those materials culture-fair may also involve a heavy visual emphasis. Additionally, it may be necessary to develop assessment materials in the first language of the child to assess whether dyslexia is present and affecting the development of skills in literacy in that first language.

Everatt, Reid and Elbeheri (2013) argue that sensitive English assessment measures are highly predictive of skills in other languages. Nevertheless, it is important to obtain measures in the child's first language as there will be differences in the development of different aspects of the reading process. Everatt *et al.* (2010) found this when undertaking research with children from the Philippines and Namibia. They found that word reading and non-word decoding developed at different rates for Filipino and Herero children in relation to English children. Despite this, Everatt and Reid (2009) suggest that phonological skills are still the main predictor of children's literacy learning in both languages.

Research in Arabic has indicated that phonological processes are predictive of reading levels amongst Arabic children, and that poor Arabic readers show weak phonological decoding and low levels of phonological awareness compared to matched normal readers (Everatt and Elbeheri 2008). It is also important to determine whether assessment procedures would be better supplemented by additional measures that focus more on the specific features of the writing system, such as an awareness of morphemic roots and patterns (Elbeheri *et al.* 2006). In terms of theory, these data are consistent with the phonological deficit viewpoint, that is, a child with a phonological deficit is likely to show problems with learning the Arabic orthography.

Kelly (2010) suggests that teachers need to consult and collaborate with people who have a sound knowledge of the cultural background of the students, as this can avoid confusing, common second-language errors of bilingual students with indicators of dyslexia. She suggests that these can sometimes overlap: as in the case of left–right confusion in Urdu, which is written from right to left, and with auditory discrimination with Punjabi speakers, who may have difficulty distinguishing 'p' from 'b'.

Guise and Reid (2016), Guise *et al.* (2016) and Reid (2011) highlight the importance of the information obtained from parents, as they will have a more complete picture of their child in a range of settings, including those not involving language skills. Guise and Reid indicate that it is important for teachers to be alerted if the child has a lack of interest in books, a discrepancy between listening comprehension and reading skills, difficulties in acquiring automaticity or difficulties with balance, as well as persistent problems in phonological awareness despite adequate exposure to English.

Guise and Reid suggest that when it is known that English is an additional language, extra information should be requested that can inform teachers about the child's competence in English, and in his or her first, and other languages. Specifically, we need to find out:

- What is the child's first language?
- How long has the child been speaking English?
- What other languages does the child speak?
- How much, and what level of education, has been in English?
- What language is spoken by the child's parents or guardians?
- What language is spoken at home, with siblings, and with friends?

It is crucial to establish at this stage that the child has sufficient skills in English to be able to understand and carry out test instructions. Some guidance on the possible effects of the student's exposure to English is provided by the UK SpLD Working Group 2005/DfES (Department for Education and Skills) Guidelines:

> Where the child's overall experience of English has been less than seven years, some impact on syntax, vocabulary and comprehension is generally to be expected. Where first exposure to English was after the age of seven, some impact on phonology and pronunciation is generally to be expected. However, much will depend on the quality and quantity of English experience during formative years. (SpLD Working Group 2005/DfES Guidelines, p.12)

Assessing non-verbal intelligence

Guise and Reid report on a number of tests that can provide information on non-verbal intelligence, and this is an important element in assessing bilingual children. The Comprehensive Test of Nonverbal Intelligence (2nd edn) (CTONI-2) (Hammill, Pearson and Wiederhol 2009) is an individually administered measure of non-verbal reasoning, and starts at age 6, so it can at least be used in the early years.

The CTONI-2 measures analogical reasoning, categorical classification and sequential reasoning, using six subtests in two different contexts: pictures of familiar objects (e.g., people, toys, animals) and geometric designs (unfamiliar sketches and drawings). The six subtests are: pictorial analogies, geometric analogies, pictorial categories, geometric categories, pictorial sequences, and geometric sequences.

The Wechsler Nonverbal Scale of Ability (WNV) (Wechsler and Naglieri 2006) is a non-verbal measure of ability for culturally and linguistically diverse groups. This test starts at age 4, which is excellent for pre-school. The full battery includes subtests on matrices, object assembly (visual organisation), coding (speed), recognition, spatial span and picture arrangement (visual sequencing).

These tests are language- and culture-free tests of intelligence, and it is therefore possible for the bilingual learner to score above average in these tests, but below average in the linguistic tests. It is therefore extremely important to utilise non-verbal intelligence tests with bilingual children.

Listening skills

The development of listening skills can help to develop auditory processing skills, and some strategies that help with this include:

- ensuring that directions are clear and concise

- avoiding multiple commands

- making sure the child understands before beginning the task

- telling the child to get ready to listen or say his or her name first

- asking the child to repeat the instructions given to him or her

- playing listening bingo (such as phonic bingo).

It is important to consider access to culturally and linguistically appropriate materials, as well as engaging in constructive communication with parents, and fostering good home/school/community links.

An interesting point is made by Fawcett (2016) who suggests that by the end of reception year the chances of showing a good level of development in EAL children is 10 per cent lower than their peers, but this gap decreases with age, with greater progress between the ages of 7 and 16. She cites the report by Strand (2015) which suggests that poor white pupils are now the lowest achieving, with only 32 per cent achieving good GCSE results (defined as five A*–C including English and Maths), whereas the Chinese, Indian and Bangladeshi groups were amongst the highest achieving. There is little doubt, as Siegel argues, that early intervention can make a significant difference, but before that can take place, high-risk children also need to be identified as early as possible.

Gray (2016) provides sound advice from the SENCo's perspective. She highlights that pupils with EAL are growing in number in English schools, and cites the figures published in a report by Professor Steve Strand at the University of Oxford (2015), that the numbers have doubled from 7.6 per cent in 1997 to 16.2 per cent in 2013. She also indicates that EAL students begin their primary schooling with lower achievement than their first language English, and presents a strong case for a screening and identification system that ensures that the 'assess' part of 'Assess, Plan, Do, Review' is timely, effective and personalised.

Guise et al. (2016) cite the study by Spencer and Hanley (2003) that considered reading development in younger children aged 5–6 and found that children reading in Welsh were more skilled in both real and nonsense words, and in phoneme awareness. In terms of the lowest achievers, English readers had a greater gap between their age and their achievement, again suggesting the regular orthography of Welsh as a protective factor. However, Hanley et al. (2004) showed that this advantage had diminished by the age of 10. They conclude, however, by acknowledging that dyslexia and multilingualism is still an area that needs further work.

Developing independent learning

Independent learning is one of the most important indictors that real learning has taken place, and it is never too young to encourage this. If children can work independently, this means that they have fully understood the task. They can make decisions based on their background understanding and their capacity and experience of independent learning.

The child who repeatedly asks someone rather than tries to work through the solution him or herself can be offloading the pressure of thinking and problem-solving to someone else, or at least sharing it. At the same time perhaps they may not have acquired those skills yet that are required by the task, so they should be applauded for asking the right questions. It is a delicate balance (as indicated earlier) between supporting (using scaffolds) and encouraging independence in learning. There is now a more obvious thrust in most education systems towards problem-solving activities that encourage children to develop an understanding of things around them and how to tackle problems, but many young children do not get enough experience in this type of activity, and this has an important message for the nursery and early years classroom.

KEY POINT

Ensure that learning involves all the senses and includes social and emotional factors.

The use of computers and technology

Learning resources for young children with dyslexia can be enriched through the use of computer programs and games. This is a growing area and it is never too early for children to become familiar with iPads or laptops. The iPad in particular has excellent software available, which is increasing almost daily.

A number of companies specialise in software for children with dyslexia. One such company is iansyst Ltd.[2] It provides a full range of text to speech software using the more advanced RealSpeak® voices that are a significant improvement on previous versions, with a much more human sounding voice. Such software can be very helpful for proofreading, as it is easier to hear mistakes than to see them, and it can help to identify if any words are in the wrong place. The company iansyst Ltd recommend software such as Wordsmith v2 as it can scan and edit paper-based text and images, listen to text being read back and can help the learner explore creative writing with speech support.

---

2   See www.iansyst.co.uk and see also www.dyslexic.com

Other computer support includes the Quicktionary Reading Pen that transfers words from the page to the LCD display when scanned by the pen. The package can be upgraded to extend its capabilities in order to convert it into a translator with over 20 different languages available. It also speaks the words and can define the word when requested.

There are also a number of typing tuition programmes that can assist with the development of touch typing. These include First Keys to Literacy, which has a recommended age range of 5–9. Some of the keyboarding activities include word lists, individual letter recognition, digraphs and rhymes and picture, letter and word prompts. There is also a program called Magictype, a fun interactive program for the 6–11 age range.

Other popular programs help to organise information, such as Kidspiration® for the 5–11 age range, which helps to develop ideas.[3] Rickitt Educational Media Ltd (R-E-M) also produces computer materials specifically aimed at dyslexia, and has produced a catalogue specifically on dyslexia.[4] The CALL (Communication, Access, Literacy and Learning) Scotland centre in Edinburgh is in many ways leading the way with innovative technology. It has developed the iPad Wheel of Apps, an excellent resource for schools and parents alike.[5]

It is important to remember, however, that although computer technology is extremely beneficial, it is no substitute for individual teaching. Young children need to be appropriately socialised, and individual teaching input is one way of doing this!

- Identify the child's strengths and take the opportunity to discuss these with the child.

- Ensure that it is possible for the child to achieve some success.

- Get the environment right – try out different types of learning environment.

- Provide short tasks.

- Help the child to think visually.

---

3   See www.inspiration.com/Kidspiration

4   See www.r-e-m.co.uk

5   See www.callscotland.org.uk and see www.callscotland.org.uk/Common-Assets/ ckfinder/userfiles/files/Wheel_0f_Apps_V1_0.pdf for the Wheel of Apps.

- Accept that over-learning will be necessary – this means that instructions may also have to be repeated.

- Take time to ensure that the child has understood the task.

- Do not limit the demands of the task because of the child's low level of literacy. Look for a means of overcoming this such as the use of taped books, technology such as voice-activated software or through working in groups.

- Children with dyslexia need over-learning but they also need to time to complete tasks, and they may need more time than others.

- Try to encourage independent learning – give children the scope to make decisions and help them to have some control over their learning.

- Help children to monitor their own progress. This also helps to provide a degree of control over their own learning.

- Give an overview of new learning first before asking the child to tackle its individual aspects.

- Learning should be fun! It is important that the child with dyslexia is self-motivated to learn. This can come about through gaining success and a stress-free learning environment.

The role of parents

As indicated in this book, parents play a very important role in working with the school in supporting their child. Although home–school liaison is very important, there can be obstacles to this. Some parents may, for whatever reason, be unable to attend school regularly, and communication has to be carried out by another means that may be less effective. Additionally, some parents may not have proficiency in English and may therefore be apprehensive about attending school meetings. If possible, the school should locate volunteers who are able to speak different languages so that every language used in the nursery or school is covered.

Parents are always keen to help their child with learning and with reading in particular. It is important that they link with the school over this to ensure that the approaches used are consistent and complementary, and that the reading materials are appropriate. One such strategy that parents can use is shown below. Many parents would do this automatically without realising that it is actually an effective reading strategy. It may therefore be important for the school to put this into a structure to help parents understand its importance.

Pre-reading discussion

It is important to engage in pre-reading discussion with children before they start reading a text. There is a body of research that suggests that pre-reading discussion is one of the best predictors of a successful outcome in a reading activity. Some questions that can provide a framework for pre-reading discussion are shown below.

Pointers for pre-reading discussion

- Where does the story take place?
- Time period?
- Main characters/anything unusual about the main characters?
- How the story starts.
- What to look out for in the story.
- How does the book/story relate to the child's previous knowledge/experience?

It might be more effective if the parent reads the story first to the child and then presents some of the questions shown above to the child.

It is also a good idea to monitor comprehension and to ensure that the child has understood the key points of the book. This could be carried out at regular intervals, and for some children it will be necessary to do this at short intervals, such as after each sentence or every paragraph, depending on the child's level of reading. It is important that parents are aware of this; otherwise, the child may spend quite a bit of time and effort reading, but get very little from the book.

Parents can help by reading with their child and stopping regularly to check and make sure the child still comprehends. Then they can encourage the child to use the same strategies when they are reading alone, so that eventually the child learns to monitor their comprehension independently.

Reciprocal reading as a structure

This approach is often used by teachers in the classroom, but can also be used successfully when reading one-on-one with a parent. To begin the process of reciprocal teaching, the parent reads a few paragraphs then summarises for the child what he or she has read. The parent then clarifies any concepts that may be confusing or words that may not be understood, asks a few questions about the passage, and makes a prediction about what will happen next.

The child then takes a turn reading and goes through the same four steps of summarising, questioning, clarifying and predicting. The exact order of the steps is not important, but it may be useful to make up cue cards with visuals for each of the four.

Questions that are creative may ask the child to change the ending to a story, or ask what they would have done if they were in the same situation as one of the characters. These require children to use their imagination to think of an answer.

Reciprocal teaching is a useful strategy for parents to use when they are concerned about comprehension. Ideally, children will become independent with this approach and will eventually learn to monitor their own comprehension. Until they are able to do this, however, it is important to put strategies in place that will get the children to the point where they will automatically recognise they do not comprehend, and know what to do about it. Reciprocal reading forces them to recognise whether or not they understand what they were reading.

Communication with the school

Reid, Green and Zylstra (2008) indicated in relation to the role of parents that the key factors are:

- Self-esteem and the need for parents and the school to collaborate to help the child develop a positive self-esteem.

- The need to ensure that communication takes place as early as possible to prevent the negative effects of failure being experienced by the child.

- The issue of homework and the need to ensure a balance exists between home and school.

- The potential for a learning difficulty to be transformed into a behavioural difficulty – it is important to focus on the cause of the difficulty and not just on the symptom.

- The need to have faith that the child will succeed and enjoy family life – fun activities will help the child maintain a relaxed attitude and help to minimise anxieties that can be caused by reading difficulties.

- It is important that schools value each child and express this to the parents.

- It is important that parents are aware of the possibility that some children with dyslexia may be overshadowed by their siblings. This underlines the need to highlight the child's strengths and not to highlight their difficulties all the time.

- It is important for parents to establish support groups. For many this is crucial as it can prevent the feeling of being alone. It can also be a valuable source of information.

Parents have a key role to play in early identification. In many cases it is the parent who may alert the school to the child's literacy development. In some cases the parent may be aware of a concern before the child even starts school, particularly if there are other children in the family or relatives who have dyslexia. Parents usually know their child well and will be alert to signs of anxiety or stress when the child is learning new material. It is important that there are good links between home and school, so it may be useful to reflect on how the school can help to make home–school links more effective.

Different types of literacy

Parents need to understand that literacy involves more than reading accuracy. The experience of language is vital for a critical appreciation of literacy. For example, the social, cultural and cognitive impact of literacy could be achieved through some other medium, apart from reading, such as discussion, television or through listening. This can help to provide the child with an enriched language experience and promote the development of conceptual understanding of language and a deeper level of processing.

If access to print is a significant barrier to obtaining this language experience, other means need to be sought. Discussion and different forms of media are therefore important to help the child access enriched language experiences and deep thinking skills that they may not be able to obtain from print. It is important for parents to appreciate this, which is why effective communication with schools is so important.

Early identification

While this book has covered this area in some detail in earlier chapters, it is important to highlight this again in this chapter as, despite its high profile, it is an ongoing issue and concern. Early identification is a key factor in identifying and intervening for dyslexia. How and when identification should take place and how it can most effectively and most sensitively be conducted are matters of some debate (see Chapter 2). But there is sound evidence that early identification and intervention can lead to more appropriate and effective support for the young child.

It may not be desirable to diagnose and label a young child with a reading difficulty as dyslexic, but as early as 3 some children display behaviours that indicate that they are not developing oral language, phonological awareness and motor skills as one would expect. In this case they need to be highlighted as at risk of dyslexia.

The essence of early identification is therefore not necessarily to label but to identify those who are at risk of developing difficulties in acquiring literacy. There is no doubt that early identification is crucial and can make a significant difference to the achievement outcome of children who are at risk. Knight *et al.* (2009) provide evidence of early identification of reading difficulty along with targeted, research-based interventions improving children's chances of becoming more effective readers. The issues and questions therefore are:

- When should early identification take place?

- How should it be conducted, and by whom?

- What criteria should be used at this early stage for a diagnosis?

These questions have already been covered in Chapter 2, but it is important to reiterate here that identifying children at risk of dyslexia should be done as early as possible, and can be done even at ages 3–4.

The actual assessment process is also described in Chapter 2, but it is important not to be put off by a lack of standardised tests. Informal assessment and observation over time can be just as effective and in many cases more effective at that particular age. Additionally, there are also screening tests such as the Dyslexia Early Screening Test (DEST) (from age 3) and the Special Needs Assessment Profile (SNAP) (from age 4) that can help inform the degree of risk.

Additionally, in England and Wales, the *SEND Code of Practice* provides scope for the 'Assess, Plan, Do, Review' structure that can also be extremely useful. Other countries use similar formulas, and these can provide important information that can help with early identification and also, very importantly, link assessment with intervention.

Early identification should not be the responsibility of one teacher, or even one school, but it should be a planned and integrated activity involving parents and professionals working together in the context of both home and school.

Early identification of children at risk of literacy failure should also be accompanied by appropriate opportunities for intervention. This can be more challenging with pre-school children as the same opportunities may not be available for assessment compared to school-aged children. Yet, if early identification is to be effective, it should focus on pre-school children as well as children in early years.

There are many issues that could have been discussed here, but some of the key ones have been highlighted. The key point is that no one teacher in whatever sector of education can solve this alone. What is needed is a whole-school perspective, and school management must be engaged in the issues discussed here.

Training is also very important, and as one who has been involved in teacher training for most of my professional career, I can steadfastly vouch for its importance. Training courses can have a value-added component and allow teachers to exchange views with others from different schools, and this is extremely important. Pooling ideas and resources adds considerably to a teacher's confidence in being able to deal effectively with the issues discussed here. Dyslexia in early years is certainly an area that is extremely suitable for further training for staff.

Concluding thoughts

Although I have focused on a number of issues here, it is clear that much has been achieved in all these areas. The actual practice and provision may well vary depending on the geographical area or indeed the country, so it is important that parents and teachers are aware of these potential issues and their importance for early years education.

Chapter 10

Concluding Comments, Resources and Practical Strategies

One of the points that has become clear to me in writing this book is that *no* sector of education – pre-school, early years, primary or secondary – should be discrete and isolated. Each one lays a foundation for the next stage. The stages are not natural 'cognitive' stages but convenience divisions for administrative purposes. Many children further up the school would thrive on the strategies commonly used in nursery and early stages. Similarly and increasingly, very young children are becoming adept at using tools – particularly technology – that would normally be the preserve of older children. Age is not the key determinant of any approach but, rather, it should be readiness to learn. This is important for children with dyslexia as they may be 'ready to learn' some key parts of the curriculum well above their age but toiling in other areas and languishing well below their age.

The stage process curriculum, which indicates what children should be doing at certain ages, is not helpful for children with dyslexia – it promotes disappointment and eventually failure. A flexible curriculum with flexible targets is what is needed for children with dyslexia. They will get there in the end – that has already been shown – but only if the learning journey ensures that motivation and morale are maintained even though they may face some challenging learning experiences. This is why it is important that teacher training in all sectors is prioritised by governments and schools. Training is particularly important for early years, since research shows that early intervention is a key process that can minimise the possibility of failure, maintain motivation and self-esteem, and lead to successful outcomes and a happier school experience.

An overview of strategies

Some of the strategies that can account for a successful outcome have been interspersed throughout this book, but it is important to highlight them here again in order to emphasise their importance.

- *Small steps:* It is important to present tasks in small steps, especially since children with dyslexia may have short-term memory difficulties. In fact, one task at a time is probably sufficient. If multiple tasks are specified, a checklist might be a useful way for the child to note and self-monitor his or her progress.

- *Group work:* Children with dyslexia benefit from working with others, but it is important to plan for group work. The dynamics of the group are crucial, and children with dyslexia need to be in a group where at least one person is able to impose some form of structure to the group tasks. This can act as a modelling experience for dyslexic children. It is also important that those in the group do not overpower the dyslexic child, so someone with the ability to facilitate the dyslexic child's contribution to the group is also important. This would make the child with dyslexia feel they are contributing to the group. Even though they may not have the reading ability of the others in the group, they will almost certainly have the comprehension and problem-solving ability, so they will be able to contribute if provided with opportunities.

- *Learning styles:* This is one of the key aspects in understanding the importance of presentation of materials and how the learning situation can be manipulated to promote more effective learning. It is important to recognise that different children will have their own preferred learning style and this includes children with dyslexia. This means that there may be some similarities in how children with dyslexia learn and process information, but there will also be individual differences, and these need to be taken into account in the planning and presentation of learning.

As suggested earlier in this book, multisensory strategies are used widely in the teaching of dyslexic children. The evidence suggests that the effectiveness of these strategies is based largely on the provision of at least one mode of learning with which the learner feels comfortable. This means that if the learner has a difficulty dealing with information using the auditory channel (listening), this could perhaps be compensated for through the use of the visual mode. The use of such compensatory strategies is well documented in the literature and is a feature of teaching programmes for children with dyslexia. It is therefore logical that consideration of the learner as an individual should be extended to a holistic appreciation of the learner's individual style.

One of the most useful learning styles models is that developed by Dunn, Dunn and Price (1975–89). This identifies five principal domains and 21 elements, all of which affect student learning. It is suggested that all these elements have to be considered during the assessment process and in the subsequent planning of teaching. The five principal domains and the 21 elements across those domains are:

»   environmental (sound, light, temperature, design)

»   emotional (motivation, persistence, responsibility, structure)

»   sociological (learning by self, pairs, peers, team, with an adult)

»   physiological (perceptual preference, food and drink intake, time of day, mobility)

»   psychological (global or analytic preferences, impulsive and reflective).

On examining these, one can recognise how the elements identified can influence the performances of dyslexic learners. It must be appreciated that dyslexic children are first and foremost learners, and like any other learner will be influenced by different learning conditions. Some children with dyslexia will prefer a 'silent' environment for concentration while others may need some auditory stimuli, perhaps even music, in order to maximise concentration and performance. Similarly with 'light', individual preferences such as dim light or bright light should be recognised.

- In relation to emotional variables, two of the elements, responsibility and structure, should certainly be addressed. It has been well documented that dyslexic learners benefit from imposed structure – most of the teaching programmes recognise this and follow a highly structured formula. At the same time, however, taking responsibility for one's own learning can be highly motivating and generate success – dyslexic learners should therefore not be deprived of the opportunity to take responsibility as some may have a natural preference for responsibility and structure.

Some tips for supporting learning

- *Use of coloured paper:* There is evidence that different background colours can enhance some children's reading and attention. Some resources such as reading rulers, page overlays, tinted exercise books and monitor overlays help with visual stress.[1] Bob Hext from Crossbow Education suggests that visual stress (also known as scotopic sensitivity) is often experienced by children with dyslexia and can result in distortion of text, headaches and sore eyes.[2] Coloured overlays can improve reading experience for about 20 per cent of the population. Hext cites the research from Uccula, Enna and Mulatti (2014), who believe that up to 46 per cent of the dyslexic population are affected by this.

- *Layout:* Page layout is very important, and this should be visually appealing and not overcrowded. A coloured background is also usually preferable. Font size can also be a key factor, and should not be too small. In relation to the actual font itself, it has been suggested that Sassoon, Comic Sans and Times New Roman are the most dyslexia-friendly fonts.

---

1   See www.crossboweducation.com
2   See www.crossboweducation.com/shop-now/visual-stress-software

Dealing with tasks

- *Provide a tick list:* This can help to keep the child with dyslexia on track. It will also help the child monitor progress.

- *Break tasks into manageable chunks:* This can provide an opportunity for the learner to achieve. Children with dyslexia may have low self-esteem – they are in a position of potential failure as soon as they start school, as most learning is based on print and literacy. It is crucial therefore that they achieve and can realise that they have achieved with some tasks. It is this achievement that provides the success, which is essential to raise their self-esteem.

- *Feedback through self-articulation:* It is often a good idea to get dyslexic children to provide oral feedback of the task they have to do or as they are doing the task. This helps to monitor their comprehension.

- *Provide a sequence to help with planning:* Children with dyslexia often have difficulties in developing and following a sequence. It can be useful to provide a structure that helps to sequence learning new material. For example, in the example below, the task is for the child to provide a summary of the key points in the passage. This, however, can be too demanding a task for the dyslexic learner and indeed for many children at the early years stage. It is important, therefore, that the task is broken down into manageable chunks, and that there is a clear sequence for the learner to follow. This example can be carried out in groups, which can be helpful for all.

  » First, underline the important words in the passage.

  » Next, write them out on a separate page.

  » Then write the meaning of each word next to it.

  » Take one word at a time and indicate why it is important for the passage.

  » Once you have completed this, decide which word is the most important and say why.

» Last, give a summary of the key points in the passage. This can be done with drawings and gluing teacher-prepared words to the page.

- *Help learners prioritise their work:* Children with dyslexia can often have difficulties in prioritising their work or even the task. This can lead to them spending a lot of time on unimportant areas of the task. It can be a good idea to indicate what aspects of the task are 'very important', 'quite important' and 'less important'. It is never too early to start this, and this can be carried out with very young children. It is a good learning habit to instil in young children and can be extremely beneficial for those with dyslexia.

Writing

- *Handwriting:* There are many supports for handwriting and this is important as it is not uncommon for children with dyslexia to have handwriting problems. Crossbow Education has a catalogue of resources on handwriting including pencil grips and ergonomic pens/pencils, which can be very effective in supporting handwriting. They are available in a selection of colours, styles, materials and designs, and can suit different types of need in relation to pencil grip. For example, the following grips are available: Classic Grip, Skittle Grip, Write Grip, Dolphin Grip, Comfort Grip, Ridged Comfort Grip, Ultra Grip, Crossguard Grip, Squooshi Grip, Claw Grip (medium) and Soft Triangular Grip.[3]

- *Expressive writing:* Supports for expressive writing include providing key words, headings and subheadings and clauses that can be used for sentence expansion.

Resources

Learning through games

Games can be fun and very effective in obtaining results. Children enjoy playing games and the fun aspect can help them learn without

---

3   See www.crossboweducation.com

realising it. There are many booksellers that stock games suitable for early years. A good starter pack is the Crossbow Card Games Compendium – the games in this pack are suitable for 6 years and upwards,[4] and include six original literacy card games by Bob Hext, with extra detailed notes on when and how to use them in the classroom. The pack contains:

- Vocabulary Sentence Rummy, where children extend their vocabulary and develop their understanding of parts of speech as they compete to collect the words that go with the sentence cards that have been turned over.

- See VC, a colourful card game with clear images that illustrate every single consonant and vowel grapheme, including consonant digraphs. This teaches letter recognition, vowel and consonant differentiation, final double consonants, 'h' digraphs and encoding and decoding skills.

- Pot the Lobster, which involves collecting all the segments of the lobster to make a nonsense sentence; it is useful for those who need to work on their memory, language and reading two-syllable words.

- Vowel Digraph Triplets: 18-colour vowel digraph with sets of three, with one rhyming pair and one non-rhyming pair for each medial vowel digraph. Each sound has a key card with a picture that is repeated on the other two cards in the triplet, for visual identification of the sound. Bob Hext suggests that this is ideal for younger children.

- Wordbuilder, an onset and rime word building card game with whole word chunks. This game includes ear, ash, oil, ark – 42 common 'building block' words and 'extra go' option cards combine to make hundreds more words in this addictive spelling strategy game.

- Strike! This is based on traditional card game play and contains CVC words with consonants that can easily be reversed. It is helpful for focusing on individual letters.

---

4   See www.crossboweducation.com/shop-now/literacy-and-language/phonics-teaching-resources/phonics-teaching-resources-games/crossbow-card-game-compendium

Art and crafts

Early Years Resources®

Art and craft resources are essential in the nursery and early years and are extremely beneficial for children who may have dyslexia, because they are quite often able to excel in this area.[5] Early Years Resources® has an excellent supply of materials for art and crafts,[6] including different types of pencils and crayons, a range of painting accessories, coloured paper and card, materials for collage making, different types of textiles, aprons and splash mats, templates and stencils and 3D materials. For reading and writing they have very useful alphabet tracing boards and alphabet pathway mats as well as active phonic and number cards. For maths and number work they have a comprehensive Early Maths Progress Pack, suitable for age 3 upwards. Each pack includes Number Pebbles (number bonds to 10), Ladybugs Counting Set, Helping Young Children with Numeracy book, Crispin the Crow Puppet, Sorting Stones and Active Number Cards.[7] They also have a range of puppets that can be useful for imaginative play.

Early Minds Education Inc.

Early Minds has an excellent range of materials,[8] and their website includes a useful introduction to Project Based Learning. They suggest that Project Based Learning has been proven to create a stronger desire to learn and a better understanding of different subjects. They have focused on Project Based Learning for early learners and their parents, as they believe this creates a stronger foundation for learning. The children are able to work at their own pace and answer the questions they are most interested in. This helps to develop problem-solving skills, independence and can create an interest in other subjects and topics that may not be covered in the curriculum. The materials are delivered via a lesson video that makes it more appealing for children and their parents. They also have an excellent section on maths with a numbers 1–10 set that also contains extensions and games.

---

5   See the video by Tom West on 'Power of Dyslexic Visual Thinkers with Computer Data Visualisation: Thomas West at Embrace Dyslexia' at www.youtube.com/watch?v=BKIIruZzS2c

6   See www.earlyyearsresources.co.uk/art-craft-c338

7   See www.earlyyearsresources.co.uk/numeracy-c46/early-maths-progress-pack-p46198

8   See www.earlyminds.com

Resources that may be suitable for pre-school and early years

Reading	Spelling	Numeracy
Posters	Letters – big, small, tactile	Egg timer, stopwatch – time
Labels	Computer apps	Scales/balance boards – weight/mass
Alphabet resources	Play sand	Number games
Alphabet arc	Play-Doh	Plastic food, beads, animals – sharing – division
Written captions	Spelling games	Shop/library, etc. – sorting
Adverts – critical reading Picture cards	Smart boards	Tape measure, ruler, measuring cups, coins, clocks, watches – measuring
Comprehension activities	Language skills	Thinking and problem-solving skills
Dictionary	Walkie talkies	Games
Poetry	Voice changer	Construction
Songs	Telephone tubes	Jigsaws
Story telling cards	Voice recorders	Maths puzzles
	Songs and story telling	
	Drama: dressing-up costumes, play telephones Dramatic play area: 'Wendy' house, carpets/mats	
Social and emotional development	Movement and coordination	Writing and pre-writing skills
Relationships	Balancing	Skills using fine motor skills
Feelings and behaviour	Climbing	Mark making skills
Self-confidence	Motor skills	Clip boards for drawing and scribbling

Listening and talking	Control of movement activities	Sign-in book to use as model for writing name
Independence	Soft play	Writing table
Values Friendship	Bikes	Picture books
Role-play		
Messy and sensory play		

Supporting Language and Literacy 0–5

Supporting Language and Literacy 0–5 (Clipson-Boyles 2010) offers practical guidance for those supporting young children's language and literacy development. It describes the important features of early language development, providing a theoretical framework with practical examples. It links directly to the EYFS and focuses on the principles of inclusion, equality, individualised learning, planning, assessment and cross-curricular working.

Supporting Writing

Supporting Writing (Edwards 2004a) has practical activities, ideas and strategies that focus on how teaching assistants can effectively enhance their pupils' literacy skills. With the focus on enhancing the writing skills of the pupil, it:

- analyses how you can develop writing skills
- offers advice and guidance on a variety of learning styles
- includes a breakdown of writing principles.

Supporting Spelling (Helping Hands)

Supporting Spelling (Helping Hands) (Edwards 2004b) is a practical book that concentrates on developing spelling skills. It offers advice and guidance on a variety of learning styles and a breakdown of spelling principles.

Dyslexia and Early Childhood: An Essential Guide to Theory and Practice

Barbara Pavey is a well-known author in the field of dyslexia, and *Dyslexia and Early Childhood* (2016) is an excellent addition to the range of books in this field. Her book draws on a great deal of current research, and essentially takes a developmental approach to understanding the needs of children with dyslexia and how these can be met in the classroom. It focuses on assessment and intervention, and also looks at the overlapping conditions such as dyspraxia as well as the role of play in the early years setting.

Concluding thoughts

Numerous resources are available for the early years. The dilemma for busy teachers is usually how to know what is best for their situation. It is a good idea to speak to someone who has used the resource or to try to get it on approval for a short period. It is important, however, to note that resources are only part of the picture. The key player is the child, and this should always be the starting point. All children are very much individuals, and it is certainly the case with dyslexia that one size does not fit all. Glean as much information from an assessment as possible, and use this to help in selecting resources.

One of the crucial points that has been reiterated throughout this book is that dealing with dyslexia in the early years is not the responsibility of one person – it is a whole-school responsibility, and this is absolutely vital. Some barriers that can hinder effective intervention have been mentioned in this book, but collaboration and cooperation between all involved – child, parents, teacher and school management – are essential. All are important and all must be considered.

There is no doubt that the early years is an important point in the school system as this is where the foundations for learning are established. It is surely important to get it right at this point and to ensure that children at risk of dyslexia receive the assessment, monitoring and intervention that are essential if they are to become effective and successful learners.

Appendix: Resources Grid

Resource/website	Publisher	Type	Review
Reading			
Spelling			
Numeracy			
Language			
Comprehension			

Resource/website	Publisher	Type	Review
Writing/pre-writing			
Movement and coordination			
Social and emotional			
Thinking and problem-solving			

Glossary of Terms

ADHD Children with ADHD (attention-deficit hyperactivity disorder) will have a short attention span and tend to work on a number of different tasks at the same time. They will be easily distracted and may have difficulty settling in some classrooms, particularly if there are a number of competing distractions. It is also possible for some children to have attention difficulties without hyperactivity (referred to as attention deficit disorder, ADD).

Auditory discrimination Many children with dyslexia can have difficulties with auditory discrimination. This refers to difficulties in identifying specific sounds and in distinguishing these sounds with other similar sounds. This can be associated with the phonological difficulties experienced by children with dyslexia (see phonological difficulties). Hearing loss or partial and intermittent hearing loss can also be associated with auditory discrimination.

Automaticity This refers to the situation when the learner obtains a degree of mastery over the skill or information that is being learned. In the case of reading this would be automatic word recognition without the need to actively decode the word, although it would also be important for the learner to achieve automaticity in decoding so that he or she would know automatically how to decode a new word. It refers to any skill that has to be learned.

Cognitive This refers to the learning and thinking process. It is the process that describes how learners take in information and how they retain and understand the information.

Decoding This refers to reading processing and specifically to the breaking down of words into individual sounds.

Differentiation This is the process of adapting materials and teaching to suit a range of learners' abilities and level of attainments. Usually differentiation refers to the task, teaching, resources and assessment. Each of these areas can be differentiated to suit the needs of individuals or groups of learners.

Dyscalculia This describes children and adults who have difficulties in numeracy. This could be due to difficulties in computation of numbers, remembering numbers or reading the instructions associated with number problems.

Dysgraphia This is difficulties in handwriting. Some children with **dyspraxia** (see below) and who are **dyslexic** may also show signs of dysgraphia. Children with dysgraphia will benefit from lined paper as they have visual/spatial problems and may have an awkward pencil grip.

Dyslexia Refers to difficulties in accessing print but also other factors such as memory, processing speed, sequencing, directions, syntax, spelling and written work which can also be challenging. Children with dyslexia often have phonological difficulties that result in poor word attack skills. In many cases they require a dedicated one-to-one intervention programme.

Dyspraxia This refers to children and adults with coordination difficulties. It can also be described as developmental coordination disorder (DCD).

Eye tracking This is the skill of being able to read a line and keep the eyes on track throughout the line. Children with poor eye tracking may omit lines or words on a page. Sometimes masking a part of a line or page or using a ruler can help with eye tracking.

Information processing This is a process that describes how children and adults learn new information. It is usually described as a cycle – input, cognition and output. Children with dyslexia can often have difficulties at all the stages of information processing and dyslexia can be referred to as a difficulty or a difference in information processing.

Learning disabilities This is a general term to describe the range of specific learning difficulties such as dyslexia, dyspraxia, dyscalculia and dysgraphia. Often referred to as LD, it is not equated with intelligence and children with LD are usually in the average to above average intelligence range.

Learning styles This can describe the learner's preferences for learning, which can be using visual, auditory, kinaesthetic or tactile stimuli, but it can also relate to environmental preferences such as sound, the use of music when learning, preferences for time of day and working in pairs, groups or individually. There is a lot of literature on learning styles, but it is still seen as quite controversial, very likely because there are hundreds of different instruments, all of which claim to measure learning styles, and many learners are, in fact, quite adaptable and can adapt to different types of learning situations and environments. Nevertheless, it is a useful concept to apply in the classroom, particularly for children with learning disabilities, as using learning styles it is more possible to identify their strengths and to use these in preparing materials and in teaching.

Long-term memory This is used to recall information that has been learned and needs to be recalled for a purpose. Many children with dyslexia can have difficulty with long-term memory as they have not organised the information they have learned, and recalling it can be challenging as they may not have enough cues to assist with recall. Study skills programmes can help with long-term memory.

Metacognition This is the process of thinking about thinking, that is, being aware of how one learns and how a problem was solved. It is a process-focused approach and one that is necessary for effective and efficient learning. Many children with dyslexia may have poor metacognitive awareness because they are unsure of the process of learning. For this reason study skills programmes can be useful.

Multiple intelligence First developed by Howard Gardener in the early 1980s in his book *Frames of Mind* it turns the conventional view of intelligence on its head. Gardener provides insights into eight intelligences and shows how the educational and social and emotional needs of all children can be catered for through the use of these intelligences. Traditionally intelligence has been equated with school success, but often this focuses predominantly on the verbal and language aspects of performance. Gardener's model is broader than that, which indicates that the traditional view of intelligence may be restrictive.

Multisensory This refers to the use of a range of modalities in learning. In this context multisensory usually refers to the use of visual, auditory, kinaesthetic and tactile learning. It is generally accepted that children with dyslexia need a multisensory approach that utilises all of these modalities.

Neurological This refers to brain-associated factors, which could be brain structure, that is, the different components of the brain or brain processing, and how the components interact with each other. The research in dyslexia shows that both brain structure and brain processing factors are implicated in dyslexia.

Peer tutoring This is when two or more children work together and try to learn from each other. It may also be the case that an older, more proficient learner is working with a younger, less accomplished learner and the younger one is the tutee and the older the tutor.

Phonological awareness This refers to the processing of becoming familiar with the letter sounds and letter combinations that make the sounds in reading print. There are 44 sounds in the English language and some sounds are very similar. This can be confusing and challenging for children with dyslexia, and they often get the sounds confused or have difficulty in retaining and recognising them when reading or in speech.

Specific learning difficulties This refers to the range of difficulties experienced that can be of a specific nature such as reading, coordination, spelling or handwriting. There are quite a number of specific learning difficulties and they can be seen as being distinct from general learning difficulties. In the latter case children with general learning difficulties usually find most areas of the curriculum challenging and may have a lower level of comprehension than children with specific learning difficulties.

Working memory This is the first stage in short-term memory. It involves the learning and holding of information in a short-term store and carrying out a processing activity simultaneously. This can be solving a problem, reading instructions or merely walking around. Working memory is when one or more stimuli is held in memory for a short period of time. Children with dyslexia often experience difficulties with working memory as they have difficulty in holding a number of different pieces of information at the same time.

Further Resources

General
International
Dyslexia International Country Directory: www.dyslexia-international.org/country-directory

North America, South America and Canada
International Dyslexia Association (IDA): www.interdys.org

Learning Disabilities Association of America: www.ldaamerica.org

Dyslexic Advantage: www.dyslexicadvantage.org

Caribbean
Caribbean Dyslexia Association & Centre: www.cpdcngo.org/cpdc/index.php?option=com_content&view=frontpage&Itemid=77

Teacher training courses
Brazil
Special Needs Education in Brazil: www.angloinfo.com/brazil/how-to/page/brazil-family-schooling-education-special-needs

Brazilian/Portuguese adaptation of Dyslexia Early Screening Test: www.scielo.br/scielo.php?script=sci_arttext&pid=S2317-17822015000300301

Canada
Canadian Academy of Therapeutic Tutors (CATT): Principal body for Orton-Gillingham training and professional development. Informative website with information on Orton-Gillingham training, tutor referral and events list (www.ogtutors.ca).

REACH Orton-Gillingham Learning Centre Inc.: An academic remediation centre and Orton-Gillingham training centre that was formed to assist individuals who are struggling to learn to read or spell. The main centre is in North Vancouver, Canada (www.reachlearningcentre.com).

Canada Dyslexia Association: Has information available in English and French (www.dyslexiaassociation.ca).

Learning Disabilities Association of British Columbia: www.ldabc.ca

The International Dyslexia Association, Ontario Branch: www.idaontario.com/dyslexia_ONBIDA_resources.html

Australia

Australian Dyslexia Association (ADA): http://dyslexiaassociation.org.au

SPELD Victoria Inc.: www.speldvic.org.au

SPELD SA: www.speld-sa.org.au

SPELD NSW: www.speldnsw.org.au

SPELD (TAS) Inc.: speldtasmania@bigpond.com

SPELD WA: speld@opera.iinet.net.au

The Dyslexia-SPELD Foundation of WA Inc.: www.dyslexia-speld.com

SPELD QLD: www.speld.org.au

Fun Track Learning Centre (Mandy Appleyard): www.funtrack.com.au

New Zealand

SPELD New Zealand: www.speld.org.nz

Dyslexia Foundation of New Zealand: www.dyslexiafoundation.org.nz

Dyslexia Support Taupo: www.facebook.com/pages/Dyslexia-Support-Taupo/157297897675835

Europe

European Dyslexia Association (EDA): www.eda-info.eu

Denmark

Danish Dyslexia Association: www.ordblind.com

Greece

Greek Dyslexia Association: www.dyslexia.gr

Hungary

Hungarian Dyslexia Association: www.diszlexia.hu

Italy

Associazione Italia Dislessia: www.dislessia.it

Luxembourg

Dyspel asbl: www.dyspel.org

Republic of Ireland

Dyslexia Association of Ireland: www.dyslexia.ie

Sweden

Swedish Dyslexia Association: www.dyslexiforeningen.se

UK

Dr Gavin Reid: www.drgavinreid.com

Dr Jennie Guise, Dysguise Ltd: Dysguise provides full psychological assessments that highlight strengths in children and adults. They identify the strong points that can help people achieve their potential. They also conduct consultancy at all stages of education and carry out workplace assessment and provide advice to employers. They also assess for other related specific learning difficulties including dyscalculia (difficulties with numbers), dyspraxia (which includes coordination difficulties) and dysgraphia (difficulties with handwriting) (see www.dysguise.com/about/definitions). A team of professional associates across Scotland carries out assessments that help people make the most of their skills and realise their learning potential (see www.dysguise.com/about/associates). They provide full assessments that help identify individual strengths and weaknesses and the particular level of support people might need. This can often be the start of a more positive journey through learning and through life in general. This unique model of assessment for children, students and adults offers quality and consistency, and an approach that is also tailored to specific needs (www.dysguise.com).

Red Rose School: Provides for the educational, emotional and social needs of no more than 48 boys and girls, aged between 7 and 16, of average and above average intelligence who experience specific learning difficulties and/or experiences that cause them to become delicate and vulnerable in a mainstream setting (www.redroseschool.co.uk; www.drsionahlannen.co.uk).

Learning Works®: An educational consultancy based in Marlborough, Wiltshire. They focus on learning and learners, from those with special educational needs and barriers to learning to the able, gifted and talented. They also aim to nurture and develop the self-belief within individuals and create opportunities for learners of all ages and abilities to achieve more than they ever believed possible. Learning Works is an innovative organisation that encourages the development of minds, creativity and individuality and helps learners to recognise what is best for themselves *and* the world (www. learning-works.org.uk).

Institute of Child Education and Psychology (ICEP) Europe: One of the most trusted leading providers of high-quality online continuing professional development (CPD) and university-validated Diploma and Master's programmes in special educational needs and psychology for teachers, parents and allied professionals who work with children and young people. Offers a wide range of programmes at all levels (www.icepe.co.uk).

Middle East

Israel

International Dyslexia Association: www.dyslexiaida.org

Kuwait

Center for Child Evaluation and Teaching: www.ccetkuwait.org
Kuwait Dyslexia Association: http://q8da.com/eng/?page_id=24

Dubai

Child Early Intervention Medical Center, Dubai (CEIMC): A highly specialised centre focusing on all aspects of child development, from birth to 18 years. It offers developmental and psychological assessments, therapy services, special needs support and a variety of programmes for children who require early intervention in learning or behaviour. It has a unique approach that emphasises individualised services for children and families incorporating the importance of health and wellness, culture, family, language, community and how they contribute to a child's overall development. It has a great deal of expertise in the field of child development and offers parents, caregivers and professionals within the community resources and tools they require for successful intervention (http://childeimc.com).

Asia

Hong Kong

Dyslexia Association (Hong Kong): www.dyslexia.org.hk

Hong Kong Association for Specific Learning Difficulties: www.asld. org.hk

Japan

Japan Dyslexia Society: info@npo-edge.jp

Singapore

Dyslexia Association of Singapore: www.das.org.sg

Africa

Egypt

Lighthouse Learning Centre (LLC), Cairo: www.llcegypt.com

Ghana

Crossroads Dyslexic Centre: One of the functions of a local dyslexic centre is to support and empower people with dyslexia and their families (contact joybanad@yahoo.com)

South Africa

South African Association for Learning and Educational Differences (SAALED): www.saaled.org.za

The Remedial Foundation: PO Box 32207, Braamfontein 2017, Johannesburg, SA

Uganda

Rise and Shine Dyslexia Organization (RASDO): PO Box 2882, Kampala, Uganda

Organisations

Arts Dyslexia Trust: http://artsdyslexiatrust.org

Creative Learning Company New Zealand: www.creativelearningcentre.com

Dyslexia Association of Ireland: www.dyslexia.ie

Northern Ireland Dyslexia Association: www.nida.org.uk

Dyslexia Advantage: www.dyslexicadvantage.org

Institute for Neuro Physiological Psychology (INPP): www.inpp.org.uk

Dr Loretta Giorcelli, a well-known international consultant: www.doctorg.org

PenFriend: www.penfriend.biz

TextHelp™: www.texthelp.com

Teaching Handwriting, Reading and Spelling Skills (THRASS): www.thrass.co.uk

Literacy

National Literacy Trust: www.literacytrust.org.uk/resources/practical_resources_info/332_archive_resource-the_national_strategies

Topping, K. (2001) *Thinking, Reading, Writing: A Practical Guide to Paired Reading with Peers, Parents and Volunteers*. New York and London: Continuum Publications

iMindMap, Buzan Centres Ltd: https://imindmap.com

Crossbow Education: www.crossboweducation.com

iansyst Ltd: www.iansyst.co.uk

PRO-ED, Inc., a leading publisher of nationally standardised tests: www.proedinc.com/customer/default.aspx

Pearson Clinical Assessment: www.pearsonassess.com

European Dyslexia Association: www.eda-info.eu

SEN Books

EdTech Software Ltd: www.edtech.ie

EU Specific Learning Disabilities Policy – European project: www.youtube.com/watch?v=e2tEBq2oJ1E

Outside the Box Learning Resources: www.otb.ie

Scanning Pens Shop: www.scanningpenshop.com

WordsWorth Learning: www.wordsworthlearning.com

Other websites

American Montessori Society: A not-for-profit organisation based in New York (https://amshq.org).

The British Dyslexia Association (BDA) indicates that it is the voice of dyslexic people and aims to influence government and other institutions to promote a dyslexia-friendly society that enables dyslexic people of all ages to reach their full potential. The BDA promotes early identification of SpLD and support in schools to ensure that there are maximum opportunities available for learners with dyslexia. In November 2007, at the BDA Annual General Meeting, members agreed the policy on early identification of SpLD. It is a very influential lobbying body and its campaign includes:

- encouraging schools to work towards becoming dyslexia-friendly

- reducing the number of dyslexic young people in the criminal justice system

- enabling dyslexic people to achieve their potential in the workplace.

It is also the main accreditation body for approved courses (www.bdadyslexia. org.uk).

Crickweb: Free interactive resources (www.crickweb.co.uk).

Dyslexia Action: A national dyslexia charity with 40 years' experience in providing support to people with literacy and numeracy difficulties, dyslexia and other specific learning difficulties. Dyslexia Action provides free advice through their learning centres and they also offer free advice and resources via their website. They provide dyslexia and specific learning difficulty testing and offer a range of assessment options from a short screening assessment to a full diagnostic assessment. Their learning centres offer specialist tuition, short skills courses and catch-up clubs to help develop literacy and numeracy skills or other needs. Courses are also available for parents to help them in supporting their children with literacy and numeracy difficulties, dyslexia and other specific learning difficulties. Their online shop offers a variety of products designed to support individuals, including Units of Sound, an online literacy intervention programme developed by Dyslexia Action (www.dyslexiaaction.org.uk).[1]

Dyslexia Scotland: A page on resources includes useful links throughout Scotland. It also has an excellent helpline (www.dyslexiascotland.org.uk).

The Dyslexia Shop: This has a wide range of book, resources and games including software for children with dyslexia of all ages. For example, they have My First and Second Reading Activity Book that would be suitable for early years. They also have Fun with Phonics and several activity books on handwriting (www.thedyslexiashop.co.uk/dyslexia-books/reading-writing-and-spelling.html).

Dyslexia Teacher: Useful information about the impact of diet on dyslexia (www.dyslexia-teacher.co.uk).

eArete: A UK-based virtual learning environment and EYFS software supplier that provides educational organisations such as nurseries, primary and secondary schools and universities with an online management system to organise and coordinate all aspects of its organisation. Its EYFS software is designed for those that have early years as part of their organisation, or are perhaps an independent nursery/pre-school. Their EYFS system includes a digital online system – custom design available; progress tracking – real-time tracking of each child showing their progress; multiple observations and assessments; and a full government-based framework, which is easily updated when government changes are made; online availability to parents rules out the necessity for printing (www.earete.co.uk).

---

1   See www.unitsofsound.com

Earlychildhood NEWS: Provides professional resources for teachers and parents (www.earlychildhoodnews.com).

Easy Learn: Provides worksheets and other aids. Big phonics workbooks give quality resources to supplement early years lessons (www.easylearn. co.uk).

Education Scotland: Contains a useful section on early years resources (www.educationscotland.gov.uk).

Everybody Learns: Lexia is an effective home reading course with excellent support (www.everybodylearns.co.uk).

Get Ready to Read: Skill building activities (activity cards) designed to support educators, parents and young children in the development of literacy skills in the years before kindergarten. It has a wide range of reading materials for early years and nursery. These include Building Literacy Every Day, Getting the Most out of Picture Books, Promoting Family Literacy, Getting Ready to Read – including literacy checklists and tips for preventing reading and writing failure. It also has a Getting Ready for Maths category for early years (www.getreadytoread.org).

The Green Board Game Co.: All the games are made from at least 70 per cent recycled materials and are all recyclable and include the BrainBox series (see below) (www.greenboardgames.com).

The Helen Arkell Dyslexia Centre gives people with dyslexia the tools they need to learn in their own way. They train dedicated professionals and help parents to nurture their children and employers to support their staff. They advocate technologies that help spelling, reading, grammar, memory and organisation so that many of the dyslexic hurdles are removed. They believe that in tomorrow's world, creativity and attitude will be key to success. The Centre offers dyslexia support and advice to anyone who may need it, whether they think they have dyslexia or care for someone who may have dyslexia. Children and adults alike are supported and offered dyslexia assessments, consultations (for children or adults) and specialist tuition. They also provide high-quality dyslexia training for teachers and teaching assistants, in-service training for schools and colleges, and dyslexia testing, offering a range of assessment options from a short screening assessment, teacher assessments to full diagnostic psychologist assessments (www. helenarkell.org.uk).

Learning Development Aids (LDA): Many excellent resources are available to order online, including Assessment Cubes, activities to develop Learning Skills, Goal Maker and Quality Circle Time (www.LDAlearning. com).

Letters and Sounds: Excellent free resources for all early years (www. letters-and-sounds.com).

Memory Booster Unlimited: Games to boost working memory (www. dyslexiaactionshop.co.uk/lucidmemoryboosterstandardunlimiteds itelicence. html#.V-AHm7XBcos).

National Literacy Trust: Contains some excellent free resources and also has a full range of resources available (www.literacytrust.org.uk).

Parentbooks: A distributor for the Reggio Emilia book and for resources in Canada (www.parentbooks.ca).

Professional Association for Childcare and Early Years (PACEY): Includes good sections on games/toys and CDs/DVDs (www.pacey.org.uk).

Reading Rockets: Reading adventure packs, children's books and authors (www.readingrockets.org).

Reggio Children: Includes information on the Reggio Emilia Approach (www.reggiochildren.it).

Scuoli e Nidi d'Infanzia: Provides details of the Reggio Emilia Approach (www.scuolenidi.re.it).

Smart Kids: Has an excellent bank of resources to buy online to cover all aspects of early years work. For phonics it has the popular Smart Chute, Phonics Readers, Phonic Screen Check, Smart Phonics and magnetic resources (www.smartkids.co.uk). For numeracy it has excellent resources for early years, which include Counting Cans, Number Caterpillars, 12 & 24 Hour Flip Chart and Olympian Number Line Board Games (www.smartkids. co.uk/collections/numeracy).

Special Educational Needs (SEN) Books: One of the largest and most established book publishers and stockists in the UK. It has an impressive catalogue, including the early years. It is a specialist bookshop covering the whole range of SEN (www.senbooks.co.uk).

Time 4 Learning: Online materials with a self-paced programme (www. time4learning.com).

TTS Group Ltd: The Early Years section is broken down into clear subsections for easy access to all aspects of early years education (www. tts-group.co.uk).

Twinkl Educational Publishing: Some free resources. Other resources are also available including PowerPoints and worksheets (www.twinkl.co.uk).

References

Alloway, T. P. (2011) 'A comparison of working memory profiles in children with ADHD and DCD.' *Child Neuropsychology 21*, 1–12.

Alloway T. P., Seed, T. and Tewolde, F. (2016) 'An investigation of cognitive overlap in working memory profiles in children with developmental disorders.' *International Journal of Educational Research 75*, 1–6.

APA (American Psychiatric Association) (2013) *Diagnostic and Statistical Manual of Mental Disorders* (5th edn) (DSM-5 TR). Washington, DC: APA.

Ayres, A. J. (1979) *Sensory Integration and the Child*. Los Angeles, CA: Western Psychological Services.

Baddeley, A. (1986) 'Working memory.' *Science 255*, 556–559.

Bardige, B. (2005) *At a Loss for Words: How America Is Failing Our Children and What We Can Do About It*. Philadelphia, PA: Temple University Press.

BDA (British Dyslexia Association) (2015) *The Science Behind Dyslexia – Position Statement*. Bracknell: BDA. Available at www.bdadyslexia.org.uk, accessed on 13 September 2016.

Becker, J., Czamara, D., Scerri, T. S., Ramus, F., Csépe, V., Talcott, J. B. *et al.* (2014) 'Genetic analysis of dyslexia candidate genes in the European cross-linguistic NeuroDys cohort.' *European Journal of Human Genetics 22*, 675–680. Available at www.dpag.ox.ac.uk/team/group-leaders/john-stein, accessed on 6 October 2015.

Biedermanet, J., Faraone, S. V., Kennan, K., Knee, D. and Tsuang, M. T. (1990) 'Family genetic and psychosocial risk factors in DSM-III attention deficit disorder.' *Journal of the American Academy of Child and Adolescent Psychiatry 29*, 526–533.

Bishop, D. V. M. and Snowling, M. J. (2004) 'Developmental dyslexia and specific language impairment: Same or different.' *Psychological Bulletin 130*, 858–886.

Blythe, P. (2001) Personal communication.

Blythe, P. and Goddard, S. (2000) *Neuro-Physiological Assessment Test Battery*. Chester: Institute for Neuro-Physiological Psychology (INNP).

Bowers, P. G. and Wolf, M. (1993) 'Theoretical links among naming speed, precise timing mechanisms and orthographic skill in dyslexia.' *Reading and Writing: An Interdisciplinary Journal 5*, 69–85.

BPS (British Psychological Society) (1999) *Dyslexia, Literacy and Psychological Assessment*. Leicester: BPS.

Brooks, G. (2013) *What Works for Children and Young People with Literacy Difficulties? The Effectiveness of Intervention Schemes* (4th edn). London: The Dyslexia-SpLD Trust.

Brown, B. V. and Bogard, K. (2007) 'Pre-kindergarten to 3rd grade (PK3) school based resources and third grade outcomes.' *Cross Currents (Child Trends Data Bank) 5*, 1–7.

Burden, R. L. (2002) 'A Cognitive Approach to Dyslexia: Learning Styles and Thinking Skills.' In G. Reid and J. Wearmouth (eds) *Dyslexia and Literacy, Theory and Practice* (pp.271–284). Chichester: Wiley.

Burdette, P. (2007) *Response to Intervention as it Relates to Early Intervening Services: Recommendations*. Alexandria, VA: Project Forum at National Association of State Directors of Special Education (NASDSE). Available at http://nasdse.org/DesktopModules/DNNspot-Store/ ProductFiles/26_515e0af4-52a4-435f-b1be-505438639cb4.pdf, accessed on 13 September 2016.

Burroughs-Lange, S. (2008) *Comparison of Literacy Progress of Young Children in London Schools: A Reading Recovery Follow up Study*. London: Institute of Education, University of London.

Buzan, T. (2005) *Mind Maps for Kids*. Buzan Centre, UK. Available at www.tonybuzan.com, accessed on 13 September 2016.

Came, F. (2007) Personal communication.

Came, F. and Reid, G. (2008) *Concern, Assess and Provide (CAP it All)*. Marlborough: Learning Works.

Caplan, M., Bark, C. and McLean, B. (2012) *Helen Arkell Spelling Test Version 2 (HAST-2)*. Farnham: Helen Arkell Dyslexia Centre.

Caravolas, M., Lervåg, A., Mousikou, P., Efrim, C., Litavský, M., Onochie-Quintanilla, E. *et al.* (2012) 'Common patterns of prediction of literacy development in different alphabetic orthographies.' *Psychological Science 23*, 678–686.

Cecchini, M. E. (no date) 'How dramatic play can enhance learning.' *Earlychildhood NEWS*. Available at www.earlychildhoodnews.com/earlychildhood/article_view.aspx?ArticleID=751, accessed on 19 September 2016.

Chall, J. S. and Popp, H. M. (1996) *Teaching and Assessing Phonics: Why, What, When, How, A Guide for Teachers*. Cambridge, MA: Educators Publishing Service.

Clipson-Boyles, S. (2010) *Supporting Language and Literacy 0–5: A Practical Guide for the Early Years Foundation Stage*. London: David Fulton Publishers.

Coffield, M., Riddick, B., Barmby, P. and O'Neill, J. (2008) 'Dyslexia Friendly Primary Schools: What Can We Learn from Asking the Pupils?' In G. Reid, A. Fawcett, F. Manis and L. Siegel (eds) *The Sage Handbook of Dyslexia* (pp.356–368). London: Sage Publications.

Coleman, M. R. Buysse, V. and Neitzel, J. (2006) *Recognition and Response: An Early Intervening System for Young Children at Risk of Learning Disabilities*. Available at www.ldonline.org/article/ Recognition_and_Response%3A_An_Early_Intervening_System_for_Young_Children_At-Risk_for_Learning_Disabilities?theme=print, accessed on 13 September 2016.

Cowling, H. and Cowling, K. (1998) *Toe by Toe: Multisensory Manual for Teachers and Parents*. Bradford: Toe by Toe.

Crombie, M. (2002) 'Dealing with Diversity in the Primary Classroom – A Challenge for the Class Teacher.' In G. Reid and J. Wearmouth (eds) *Dyslexia and Literacy: Theory and Practice*. Chichester: Wiley.

Crombie, M. (2016) 'Literacy.' In L. Peer and G. Reid (eds) *Special Education Needs: A Guide for Inclusive Practice* (2nd edn) (pp.168–182). London: Sage Publications.

Crombie, M. and Reid, G. (2009) 'The Role of Early Identification: Models from Research and Practice.' In G. Reid (ed.) *The Routledge Companion to Dyslexia* (pp.71–79). Abingdon: Routledge.

Davies, A. (1996) *Teaching Handwriting, Reading and Spelling System (THRASS)*. London: Collins Educational.

Denckla, M. B. and Rudel, R. G. (1976) 'Rapid "automatised" naming (RAN): Dyslexia differentiated from other learning disabilities.' *Neuropsychologia 14*, 471–479.

Dennison, G. E. and Dennison, P. E. (1989) *Educational Kinesiology Brain Organisation Profiles*. Glendale, CA: Edu-Kinesthetics.

Dennison, G. E. and Dennison, P. E. (2001) *Brain Gym® Course Manual*. Glendale, CA: Educ. Kinesthetics.

Dennison, P. E. and Hargrove, G. (1985) *Personalized Whole Brain Integration*. Glendale, CA: Educ. Kinesthetics.

Department of Education and Skills (Ireland) (2001) *Report of the Task Force on Dyslexia*. Dublin: Department of Education and Skills. Available at www.sess.ie/sites/default/files/Dyslexia_ Task_Force_Report_0.pdf, accessed on 8 October 2015.

DfE (Department for Education) (2014a) *The Early Years Foundation Stage (EYFS)*. London: Her Majesty's Government.

DfE (2014b) *Early Years: Guide to the 0 to 25 SEND Code of Practice.* Available at https://www.gov.uk/government/uploads/system/uploads/attachment_data/file/350685/Early_Years_Guide_to_SEND_Code_of_Practice_-_02Sept14.pdf, accessed on 3 January 2017. London: The Stationery Office.

DfE (Department for Education) and DH (Department of Health) (2015) *Special Educational Needs and Disability Code of Practice 0–25 Years.* January. London: HM Government.

Drysdale, J. (2009) 'Overcoming the Barriers to Literacy: An Integrated, Contextual Workshop Approach.' In G. Reid (ed.) *The Routledge Companion to Dyslexia* (pp.236–247). Abingdon: Routledge.

Dyslexia Action (2014) *Units of Sound.* Version 6. Egham: Dyslexia Action. Available at www.dyslexiaactionshop.co.uk/unitsofsoundstageonebook.html#.VakH5evF_dk, accessed on 14 September 2016.

East Renfrewshire Council (1999) *Dyslexia, Policy on Specific Learning Difficulties.* July. Barrhead: East Renfrewshire Council.

Edwards, S. (2004a) *Supporting Writing.* London: David Fulton Publishers.

Edwards, S. (2004b) *Supporting Spelling (Helping Hands).* London: David Fulton Publishers.

Ehri, L. (1999) 'Phases of Development in Learning to Read Words.' In J. Oakhill and R. Beard (eds) *Reading Development and the Teaching of Reading: A Psychological Perspective* (pp.79–108). Oxford: Blackwell.

Elbeheri, G., Everatt, J., Reid, G. and al Mannai, H. (2006) 'Dyslexia assessment in Arabic.' *Journal of Research in Special Educational Needs 6*, 143–152.

Elbeheri, G., Reid, G. and Everatt, J. (2017) *Motivating Children with Specific Learning Difficulties: A Teacher's Practical Guide.* London: Routledge.

Elliott, J. G. and Grigorenko, E. L. (2014a) *The Dyslexia Debate.* New York: Cambridge University Press.

Elliott, J. G. and Grigorenko, E. L. (2014b) 'The end of dyslexia?' *The Psychologist 27*, 576–581.

Evans, A. (1989) *Paired Reading: A Report on Two Projects.* Sheffield: Division of Education, University of Sheffield.

Everatt, J. and Elbeheri, G. (2008) 'Dyslexia in Different Orthographies: Variability in Transparency.' In G. Reid, A. Fawcett, F. Manis and L. Siegel (eds) *The Sage Handbook of Dyslexia* (pp.427–438). London: Sage Publications.

Everatt, J., Ocampo, D., Veii, K., Nenopoulou, S. et al. (2010) 'Dyslexia in biscriptal readers.' In N. Brunswick, S. McDougall and P. de Mornay Davies (eds) *Reading and Dyslexia in Different Orthographies* (pp.221–245). Hove: Psychology Press.

Everatt, J., Ocampo, D., Veii, K., Nenopoulou, S. et al. (2010) 'Dyslexia in biscriptal readers.' In N. Brunswick, S. McDougall and P. de Mornay Davies (eds) *Reading and Dyslexia in Different Orthographies* (pp.221–245). Hove: Psychology Press.

Everatt, J. and Reid, G. (2009) 'Dyslexia: An Overview of Recent Research.' In G. Reid (ed.) *The Routledge Companion to Dyslexia* (pp.3–21). Abingdon: Routledge.

Everatt, J., Adams, E. and Smythe, I. (2000) 'Bilingual Children's Profiles on Dyslexia Screening Measures.' In L. Peer and G. Reid (eds) *Multilingualism, Literacy and Dyslexia. A Challenge for Educators* (pp.36–44). London: David Fulton Publishers.

Everatt, J., Reid, G. and Elbeheri, G. (2013) 'Assessment Approaches for Multilingual Learners with Dyslexia.' In D. Martin (ed.) *Researching Dyslexia in Multilingual Settings: Diverse Perspectives* (pp.18–35). Bristol: Multilingual Matters.

Fawcett, A. J. (2002) 'Dyslexia and Literacy: Key Issues for Research.' In G. Reid and J. Wearmouth (eds) *Dyslexia and Literacy, Theory and Practice.* Chichester: Wiley.

Fawcett, A. J. (2016) 'Latest Theoretical Thinking Around Dyslexia.' Paper presented at South Wales Conference for Specific Learning Difficulties. Pembrokeshire County Council, 29 February.

Fawcett, A. J. and Nicolson, R. I. (2004) *Dyslexia Early Screening Test (2nd edn) (DEST-2).* London: The Psychological Corporation.

Fawcett, A. J. and Nicolson, R. I. (2008) 'Dyslexia and the Cerebellum.' In G. Reid, A. Fawcett, F. Manis and L. Siegel (eds) *The Sage Handbook of Dyslexia* (pp.77–98). London: Sage Publications.

Fawcett, A. J., Lee, R. and Nicolson, R. I. (2014) 'Sustained benefits of a multi-skill intervention for pre-school children at risk of literacy difficulties.' *Asia Pacific Journal of Developmental Differences 1*, 62–68.

Fawcett, A. J., Nicolson, R. I. and Lee, R. (2001) *Pre-school Screening Test (PREST)*. Sidcup: Psychological Corporation.

Fitts, P. M. and Posner, M. I. (1967) *Human Performance*. Belmont, CA: Brooks Cole.

Flavell, J. H. (1979) 'Metacognition and cognitive monitoring.' *American Psychologist*, October, 906–911.

Fletcher, H. and Caplan, M. (2014) *Anyone Can Spell It: A Guide for Teachers and Parents*. Farnham: Helen Arkell Dyslexia Centre.

Frederickson, N., Frith U. and Reason, R. (1997) *Phonological Assessment Battery (PhAB)*. London: GL Assessment. Available at www.gl-assessment.co.uk/products/phonological-assessment-battery-second-edition-primary, accessed on 14 October 2016.

Frith, U. (1985) 'Beneath the Surface of Developmental Dyslexia.' In K. E. Patterson, J. C. Marshall and M. Coltheart (eds) *Surface Dyslexia* (pp.495–515). London: Routledge & Kegan Paul.

Frith, U. (1995) 'Dyslexia: Can we have a shared theoretical framework?' *Educational and Child Psychology 12*, 1, 6–17.

Frith, U. (2002) 'Resolving the Paradoxes of Dyslexia.' In G. Reid and J. Wearmouth (eds) *Dyslexia and Literacy, Theory and Practice* (pp.45–68). Chichester: Wiley.

Gardner, H. (1985) *Frames of Mind*. New York: Basic Books.

Gathercole, S. and Alloway, T. P. (2008) *Working Memory and Learning. A Practical Guide for Teachers*. London: Sage Publications.

Geva, E. and Herbert, K. (2012) 'Assessment and Interventions in English Language Learners with LD.' In B. Wong and D. Butler (eds) *Learning about Learning Disabilities* (4th edn) (pp.271–298). San Diego, CA: Elsevier.

Gibbs, S. and Bodman, S. (2014) *Phonological Assessment Battery (2nd edn: Primary) (PhAB 2)*. London: GL Assessment. Available at www.gl-assessment.co.uk/products/phonological-assessment-battery-second-edition-primary, accessed on 14 September 2016.

Gray, A. (2016) 'English as an Additional Language (EAL), Special Educational Needs and Dyslexia: The Role of the 21st Century SENCo.' In L. Peer and G. Reid (eds) *Multilingualism, Literacy and Dyslexia: Breaking Down Barriers for Educators* (2nd edn) (pp.115–123). London: Routledge.

Gross, J. (2006) *The Long Term Costs of Literacy Difficulties*. London: KPMG Foundation.

Guise, J. and Reid, G. (2016) 'Mind Reading for Teachers: Memory, Metacognition and Effective Learning.' Paper presented at BDA International Conference, Oxford, March.

Guise, J., Reid, G, Lannen, S. and Lannen, C. (2016) 'Dyslexia and Specific Learning Difficulties: Assessment and Intervention in a Multilingual Setting.' In L. Peer and G. Reid (2015) *Multilingualism, Literacy and Dyslexia: Breaking Down Barriers for Educators*. London: Routledge.

Gustaffsson, J.-E., Hansen, K. Y. and Rosén, M. (2011) 'Effects of Home Background on Student Achievement in Reading, Mathematics and Science at the Fourth Grade TIMSS & PIRLS.' In TIMMS and PIRLS, *Relationships Report* (Chapter 4, p.181). Chestnut Hill, MA: TIMSS & PIRLS International Study Center, Lynch School of Education, Boston College. Available at http://timssandpirls.bc.edu/timsspirls2011/downloads/TP11_Chapter_4.pdf, accessed on 13 September 2016.

Hammill, D. D., Pearson, N. A. and Wiederholt, J. L. (2009) *Comprehensive Test of Nonverbal Intelligence* (2nd edn) (CTONI-2). Oxford: Pearson Clinical.

Hanley, J. R., Masterson, J., Spencer, L. H. and Evans, D. (2004) 'How long do the advantages of learning to read a transparent orthography last? An investigation of the reading skills and reading impairment of Welsh children at 10 years of age.' *The Quarterly Journal of Experimental Psychology Section A 57*, 1393–1410.

Hannaford, C. (1995) *Smart Moves. Why Learning Is Not All in Your Head*. Arlington, VA: Great Ocean.

Hannaford, C. (1997) *The Dominance Factor. How Knowing Your Dominant Eye, Ear, Brain, Hand and Foot Can Improve Your Learning*. Arlington, VA: Great Ocean.

Hart, B. and Risley, T. R. (2003) 'The early catastrophe: The 30 million word gap by age 3.' *American Educator*, Spring. Available at www.aft.org/sites/default/files/periodicals/TheEarlyCatastrophe.pdf, accessed on 13 September 2016.

Haslum, M. N. and Miles, T. R. (2007) 'Motor performance and dyslexia in a national cohort of 10 year old children.' *Dyslexia 13*, 4, 257–275.

Hatcher, P. (2001) *Sound Linkage* (2nd edn). Chichester: Wiley.

Helen Arkell Dyslexia Centre (2014) *Helen Arkell Spelling Test* (HAST). Farnham: Helen Arkell Dyslexia Centre.

Henry, G., Rickman, D., Ponder, B., Henderson, L., Mashburn, A. and Gordon, C. (2004) *The Georgia Early Childhood Study: 2001–2004 Final Report.* Atlanta, GA: Andrew Young School of Policy Studies, Georgia State University.

Henry, M. K. (2003) *Unlocking Literacy: Effective Decoding and Spelling Instruction.* Baltimore, MD: Brookes Publishing Co.

Henry, M. K. and Brickley, S. G. (eds) (1999) *Dyslexia: Samuel T. Orton and his Legacy.* Baltimore, MD: International Dyslexia Association.

Hislop, A. (2014) 'Writing Words from Pictures.' Available at www.tes.com/teaching-resource/writing-words-from-pictures-11329208, accessed on 13 September 2016.

HM Inspectorate of Education (2008) *Education for Learners with Dyslexia.* Livingston: HMI Inspectorate of Education.

Holland, K. (2010) 'Vision and Learning.' In L. Peer and G. Reid (eds) *Special Educational Needs: A Guide for Inclusive Practice* (pp.112–126). London: Sage Publications.

Holland, K. and Holland, C. (2016) 'Vision and Learning.' In L. Peer and G. Reid (eds) *Special Educational Needs: A Guide for Inclusive Practice* (2nd edn) (pp.136–151). London: Sage Publications.

Houston, M. (2004) *Dyslexia: Good Practice Guide.* Edinburgh: City of Edinburgh Council.

Hughes, L. A. and Cooper, P. (2007) *A Teacher's Guide for ADHD.* London: Sage Publications.

Jolly Learning (no date) *Jolly Phonics: Parent/Teacher Guide.* Chigwell: Jolly Learning. Available at www.lancaster.lincs.sch.uk/pdf/Parent%20Teacher%20Guide.pdf, accessed on 15 September 2016.

Jones, N. (2005) 'Children with developmental coordination disorder: Setting the scene.' in N. Jones (ed.) *Developing School Provision for Children with Dyspraxia* (Chapter 1). London: Paul Chapman.

Joshi, R. M., Dahlgren, M. and Boulware-Gooden, R. (2002) 'Teaching reading in an inner city school through a multisensory approach.' *Annals of Dyslexia 52,* 229–242.

Kaplan, B. J., Wilson, B. N., Dewey, D. M. and Crawford, S. G. (1998) 'DCD may not be a discrete disorder.' *Human Movement Science 17,* 471–490.

Keene, E. and Zimmerman, S. (2007) *Mosaic of Thought: The Power of Comprehension Strategy Instruction.* Portsmouth, NH: Heinemann.

Kelly, C. (2010) *Hidden Worlds: Young Children Learning Literacy in Multicultural Contexts.* Stoke-on-Trent: Trentham Books.

Killick, S. (2005) *Emotional Literacy: At the Heart of the School Ethos.* London: Paul Chapman.

Kirby, A. (2003) *The Adolescent with Developmental Co-ordination Disorder.* London: Jessica Kingsley Publishers.

Kirby, A. (2006) *Dyspraxia: Developmental Co-ordination Disorder.* London: Souvenir Press Ltd.

Klein, A. S. (2009) 'Different approaches to teaching: Comparing three preschool programs.' Earlychildhood NEWS. Available at www.earlychildhoodnews.com/earlychildhood/article_view.aspx?ArticleID=367, accessed on 14 September 2016.

Knight, D. F., Day, K. and Patton-Terry, N. (2009) 'Preventing and Identifying Reading Difficulties in Young Children.' In G. Reid (ed.) *The Routledge Companion to Dyslexia* (pp.61–70). Abingdon: Routledge.

Lamy, C., Barnett, W. S. and Jung, K. (2005) *The Effects of Oklahoma's Early Childhood Four Year Programme on Young Children's School Readiness.* New Brunswick, NJ: National Institute for Early Education Research (NIEER), Rutgers University.

Landon, J. (2001) 'Inclusion and Dyslexia – The Exclusion of Bilingual Learners?' In L. Peer and G. Reid (eds) *Dyslexia: Successful Inclusion in the Secondary School* (pp.182–187). London: David Fulton Publishers.

Letterland International Ltd (1997) *About Letterland '97.* Barton: Letterland International Ltd.

Lloyd, S. and Wernham, S. (1998) *Jolly Phonics.* Chigwell: Jolly Learning Ltd. Available at http://jollylearning.co.uk/overview-about-jolly-phonics/, accessed on 14 September 2016.

Long, R. and Weedon, C. (2017) *Special Needs Assessment Profile – Behaviour (SNAP-B).* London: Hodder Education [in press].

Long, R., Weedon, C. and Reid, G. (2008) *Special Needs Assessment Profile (SNAP) Together Demo CD-ROM.* London: Hodder Education.

Lynch, R. (2007) *Enriching Children, Enriching the Nation: Public Investment in High Quality Prekindergarten.* Washington, DC: Economic Policy Institute. Available at www.epi.org/publication/book_ enriching, accessed on 13 September 2016.

Macintyre, C. (2001) *Dyspraxia 5–11 (A Practical Guide).* London: David Fulton Publishers.

Macintyre, C. and McVitty, K. (2004) *Movement and Learning in the Early Years: Supporting Dyspraxia and other Difficulties.* London: Sage Publications.

Mahfoudhi, A. and Haynes, C. (2009) 'Phonological Awareness in Reading Disabilities Remediation: Some General Issues.' In G. Reid (ed.) *The Routledge Companion to Dyslexia* (pp.139–156). London: Routledge.

Mahfoudhi, A., Elbeheri, G. and Everatt, J. (2009) 'Reading and Dyslexia in Arabic.' in G. Reid (ed.) *The Routledge Companion to Dyslexia* (pp.311–320). Abingdon: Routledge.

Martin, N. and Brownell, R. (2005) *Test of Auditory Processing Skills (3rd edn) (TAPS-3).* Novato, CA: Academic Therapy Publications. Available at www.academictherapy.com/detailATP. tpl?eqskudatarq=8338-2, accessed on 14 September 2016.

Mashburn, A., Pianta, R., Hamre, B., Downer, J., Barbarin, O., Bryant, D. *et al.* (2008) 'Measures of classroom quality in prekindergarten and children's development of academic language and social skills.' *Child Development 79,* 732–749.

Mather, N., Roberts, R., Hammill, D. D. and Allen, E. A. (2008) *Test of Orthographic Competence (TOC).* Novato, CA: Academic Therapy Publications.

McDonald, S.J. (2009) *Towards a Sociology of Dyslexia: Exploring Links between Dyslexia, Disability and Social Class.* Germany: VDM Verlag Dr. Müller.

McGuiness, D. (1997) *Why Our Children Can't Read, and What We Can Do about It.* New York: Free Press.

McPhillips, M., Hepper, P. G. and Mulhern, G. (2000) 'Effects of replicating primary-reflex movements on specific reading difficulties in children: A randomised double-blind, controlled trial.' *The Lancet 355,* 537–541.

Miller Guron, L. and Lundberg, I. (2004) 'Error patterns in word reading among primary school children: A cross-orthographic study.' *Dyslexia 10,* 44–60.

Molfese, D. L., Molfese, V. J., Barnes, M. E., Warren, C. G. and Molfese, P. J. (2008) 'Familial Predictors of Dyslexia: Evidence from Preschool Children With and Without Familial Dyslexia Risk.' In G. Reid, A. Fawcett, F. Manis and L. Siegel (eds) *The Sage Handbook of Dyslexia* (pp.99–120). London: Sage Publications.

Molfese, V. J. and Molfese, D. L. (2002) 'Environmental and social influences on reading as indexed by brain and behavioural responses.' *Annals of Dyslexia 52,* 121–137.

Mosley, J. (1996) *Quality Circle Time.* Cambridge: LDA.

National Reading Panel (2000) *Teaching Children to Read: An Evidence-Based Assessment of the Scientific Research Literature on Reading and its Implications for Reading Instruction.* Washington, DC: US Department of Health and Human Services, Public Health Service, National Institutes of Health, National Institute of Child Health and Human Development. Available at www.nichd. nih.gov/publications/pubs/nrp/documents/report.pdf, accessed on 14 October 2016.

Neuman, S. B. (2006) 'The Knowledge Gap. Implications for Early Education.' In D. K. Dickenson and S. B. Neuman (eds) *Handbook for Early Literacy Research,* Vol. 2 (pp.29–40). New York: Guilford Press.

Nicolson, R. I. (2005) 'Dyslexia: Beyond the myth.' *The Psychologist 18,* 658–659.

Nicolson, R. I. (2016) 'Response to Julian Elliott.' In J. G. Elliott and R. Nicolson, *Dyslexia: Developing the Debate.* London: Bloomsbury Academic.

Nicolson, R. I. and Fawcett, A. J. (1990) 'Automaticity: A new framework for dyslexia research?' *Cognition 35,* 159–182.

O'Keefe, J. and Farrugia, J. (2016) 'Speech and Language.' In L. Peer and G. Reid (eds) *Special Educational Needs: A Guide for Inclusive Practice* (2nd edn) (pp.79–96). London: Sage Publications.

Ottley, P. and Bennett, L. (1997) *Launch into Reading Success Through Phonological Awareness Training.* Oxford: Pearson Education Ltd.

Palti, G. (2016) 'Approaching Dyslexia and Multiple Languages.' In L. Peer and G. Reid (eds) *Multilingualism, Literacy and Dyslexia: Breaking Down Barriers for Educators* (2nd edn) (pp.190–199). Abingdon: Routledge.

Pavey, B. (2016) *Dyslexia and Early Childhood: An Essential Guide to Theory and Practice.* London: David Fulton Publishers/NASEN Publications.

Pianta, R. and Hadden, D. S. (2008) *What Do We Know about the Quality of Early Education Settings: Implications for Research on Teacher Preparation and Professional Development.* Charlottesville, VA: National Center for Research on Early Childhood Education (NCRECE), University of Virginia.

Philips, S., Kelly, K. and Symes, K. L. (2013) *Assessment of Learners with Dyslexic Type Difficulties.* London: Sage Publications.

Pickering, D. (2016) 'Early years flexibility "crucial", says Minister.' *North Edinburgh News,* 20 July. Available at http://nen.press/2016/07/20/early-years-flexibility-crucial-says-minister, accessed on 13 October 2016.

Portwood, M. (2001) *Developmental Dyspraxia: A Practical Manual for Parents and Professionals.* London: David Fulton Publishers.

Portwood, M. (2002) 'School Based Trials of Fatty Acid Supplements.' Paper presented at Education Conference, Durham County Council, June.

Princiotta, D., Flanagan, K. D. and Hausken, E. G. (2006) *Findings from the Fifth Grade Follow Up of the Early Childhood Longitudinal Study, Kindergarten Class of 1998–99 (ECLS).* NCES 2006-038. Washington, DC: US Department of Education.

Ramus, F., Pidgeon, E. and Frith, U. (2003) 'The relationship between motor control and phonology in dyslexic children.' *Journal of Child Psychology and Psychiatry 44,* 712–722.

Reason, R. and Frederickson, N. (1996) 'Discrepancy Definitions or Phonological Assessment.' In G. Reid (ed.) *Dimensions of Dyslexia: Assessment, Teaching and the Curriculum* Vol. 1. Edinburgh: Moray House.

Reid, G. (2006) 'Managing Attention Difficulties in the Classroom: A Learning Styles Perspective.' In G. Lloyd, J. Stead and D. Cohen (eds) *Critical New Perspectives on ADHD* (pp.198–214). Abingdon: Routledge.

Reid, G. (2007) *Motivating Learners in the Classroom: Ideas and Strategies.* London: Sage Publications.

Reid, G. (2011) *Dyslexia: A Guide for Parents* (2nd edn). May. Chichester: Wiley.

Reid, G. (2016a) *Dyslexia: A Practitioners Handbook* (5th edn). Chichester: Wiley.

Reid, G. (2016b) *Dyslexia and Creativity in Learning Differences Handbook.* Sydney, NSW: Learning Differences Convention.

Reid, G. and Green, S. (2008) *Dyslexia: A Guide for Teaching Assistants.* London: Continuum Publications.

Reid, G. and Green, S. (2016) *100 Ideas for Primary Teachers: Supporting Children with Dyslexia.* London: Bloomsbury Education.

Reid, G. and Guise, J. (2017) *The Dyslexia Assessment.* London: Bloomsbury.

Reid, G., Davidson-Petch, L. and Deponio, P. (2004) *Scotland-wide Audit of Education Authority Early Years Policies and Provision Regarding Specific Learning Difficulties (SpLD) and Dyslexia.* Edinburgh: Scottish Executive Education Department. Available at www.gov.scot/Resource/Doc/37428/0009597.pdf, accessed on 14 October 2016.

Reid, G., Deponio, P. and Davidson-Petch, L. (2005) 'Identification, assessment and intervention – Implications of an audit on dyslexia policy and practice in Scotland.' *Dyslexia 11,* 1–14.

Reid, G., Green, S. and Zylstra, C. (2009) 'Role of Parents.' In G. Reid, A. Fawcett, F. Manis and L. Siegel (eds) *The Sage Handbook of Dyslexia* (pp.411–424). London: Sage Publications.

Reid Lyon, G. (2004) 'Dyslexia in the USA.' Keynote presentation at the British Dyslexia Association Conference, April.

Richardson, A. J. (2002) 'Dyslexia, dyspraxia and ADHD – Can Nutrition Help?' Paper presented at Education Conference, Durham County Council, June.

Richardson, A. J. and Puri, B. K. (2000) 'The potential role of fatty acids in attention deficit/hyperactivity disorder (ADHD).' *Prostaglandins, Leukotrines and Essential Fatty Acids 2000 63,* 79–87.

Rose, J. (2006) *Independent Review of the Teaching of Early Reading. Final Report.* March. London: Department for Education and Skills.

Rose, J. (2009) *The Rose Review: Identifying and Teaching Children and Young People with Dyslexia and Literacy Difficulties.* London: The Stationery Office.

Sawyer, D. J. and Bernstein, S. (2008) 'Students with Phonological Dyslexia in School-based Programs: Insights from Tennessee Schools.' In G. Reid, A. Fawcett, F. Manis and L. Siegel (eds) *The Sage Handbook of Dyslexia* (pp.312–336). London: Sage Publications.

Scerri, T. S., Paracchini, S., Morris, A., MacPhie, I. L., Talcott, J., Richardson, A. J. *et al.* (2010) 'Identification of candidate genes for dyslexia susceptibility on chromosome 18.' *PLoS One*, October 28, 5, 10, e13712. Available at http://journals.plos.org/plosone/article?id=10.1371/journal.pone.0013712, accessed on 13 September 2016.

Scottish Government, The (2008) *Early Years Framework*. Edinburgh: The Scottish Government.

Scottish Government, The (2014) *National Practice Guidance on Early Learning and Childcare*. Edinburgh: The Scottish Government. Available at www.gov.scot/Publications/2014/08/6262, accessed on 13 September 2016.

Scottish Government, The (no date) 'Definition of Dyslexia.' Edinburgh: The Scottish Government. Available at www.gov.scot/Topics/Education/Schools/welfare/ASL/dyslexia, accessed on 13 September 2016.

Sheslow, D. and Adams, W. (2003) *Wide Range Assessment of Memory and Learning* (2nd edn) (WRAML2). Oxford: Pearson Clinical. Available at www.pearsonclinical.com/psychology/products/100001702/wide-range-assessment-of-memory-and-learning-second-edition-wraml2.html, accessed on 14 September 2016.

Shiel, G. (2002) 'Literacy Standards and Factors Affecting Literacy: What National and International Assessments Tell Us.' In G. Reid and J. Wearmouth (eds) *Dyslexia and Literacy: Theory and Practice* (pp.131–145). Chichester: Wiley.

Siegel, L. (2016) 'Bilingualism and Dyslexia: The Case of Children Learning English as an Additional Language.' In L. Peer and G. Reid (eds) *Multilingualism, Literacy and Dyslexia: Breaking Down Barriers for Educators* (2nd edn) (pp.137–147). London: Routledge.

Singleton, C. (2002) 'Dyslexia: Cognitive Factors and Implications for Literacy.' In G. Reid and J. Wearmouth (eds) *Dyslexia and Literacy* (pp.115–129). Chichester: Wiley.

Snowling, M. J. (2000) *Dyslexia* (2nd edn). Oxford: Blackwell.

Sordy, B. J. (1995) 'Benefit of docosahexaenoic acid supplements to dark adaptation in dyslexia.' *The Lancet 346*, 385.

Sordy, B. J. (1997) 'Dyslexia, attention deficit hyperactivity disorder, dyspraxia – Do fatty acids help?' *Dyslexia Review 9*, 2.

Spencer, L. H. and Hanley, J. R. (2003) 'Effects of orthographic transparency on reading and phoneme awareness in children learning to read in Wales.' *British Journal of Psychology 94*, 1, 1–28.

SpLD Working Group 2005/DfES Guidelines (2005) *Assessment of SpLDs in Higher Education*. Available at www.sasc.org.uk/SASCDocuments/SpLD_Working_Group_2005-DfES_Guidelines.pdf, accessed on 14 October 2016.

Strand, S. D. L. (2015) *English as an Additional Language (EAL) and Educational Achievement in England: An Analysis of the National Pupil Database*. Oxford: Department of Education, University of Oxford.

Sure Start Children's Centres (2010) *Guidance for Identifying and Supporting Young Children with Special Educational Needs for Early Years Settings, Schools and Support Services*. Oxford: Oxfordshire County Council.

Topping, K. J. (2001a) *Peer Assisted Learning: A Practical Guide for Teachers*. Cambridge, MA: Brookline Books. Available at www.dundee.ac.uk/esw/research/resources/readon/peerassistedlearningapracticalguideforteac/, accessed on 13 September 2016.

Topping, K. J. (2001b) *Thinking, Reading, Writing: A Practical Guide to Paired Learning with Peers, Parents and Volunteers*. New York and London: Continuum International.

Torgesen, J. K. (1996) 'A Model of Memory from an Informational Processing Perspective: The Special Case of Phonological Memory.' In G. R. Lyon and N. A. Krasnegor (eds) *Attention, Memory and Executive Function* (pp.157–184). Baltimore, MD: Brookes Publishing Co.

Torgesen, J. K. (2004a) 'Avoiding the devastating downward spiral: The evidence that early intervention prevents reading failure.' *American Educator 28*, 6–19. [Reprinted in the 56th Annual Commemorative Booklet of the International Dyslexia Association, November 2005.]

Torgesen, J. K. (2004b) 'Preventing early reading failure.' *American Educator*, Fall.

Torgesen, J. K. (2005) 'Recent Discoveries on Remedial Interventions for Children with Dyslexia.' In M. J. Snowling and C. Hulme (eds) *The Science of Reading. A Handbook* (pp.521–37). Oxford: Blackwell.

Torgesen, J. K. and Bryant, P. R. (2004) *Test of Phonological Awareness (2nd edn: Plus) (TOPA-2+)*. Oxford: Pearson Clinical.

Torgesen, J. K., Morgan, S. T. and Davis, C. (1992) 'Effects of two types of phonological training on word learning in kindergarten children.' *Journal of Educational Psychology 84,* 364–370.

Torgesen, J. K., Wagner, R. K. and Rashotte, C. A. (1997) 'Prevention and remediation of severe reading disabilities: Keeping the end in mind.' *Scientific Studies of Reading 1,* 217–234.

Turner, M. and Smith, P. (2004) *Dyslexia Screener.* London: GL Assessment. Available at www.gl-assessment.co.uk/products/dyslexia-screener, accessed on 13 September 2016.

Uccula, A., Enna, M. and Mulatti (2014) 'Colors, colored overlays and reading skills.' *Frontiers in Psychology 8,* 833. Available at www.ncbi.nlm.nih.gov/pmc/articles/PMC4114255/, accessed on 13 September 2016.

Ulmer, C. and Timothy, M. (2001) 'How Does Alternative Assessment Affect Teachers' Practice? Two Years Later.' Paper presented at the 12th European Conference on Reading, Dublin, Ireland, 1–4 July.

Vellutino, F. R., Fletcher, J. M., Snowling, M. J. and Scanlon, D. M. (2004) 'Specific reading disability (dyslexia): What have we learnt in the past four decades?' *Journal of Child Psychology and Psychiatry 45,* 1, 2–40.

Venezky, R. (1999) *The American Way of Spelling: The Structure and Origins of American English Orthography.* New York: Guilford Press.

Wagner, R. K., Torgesen, J. K. and Rashotte, C. A. (1999) *Comprehensive Test of Phonological Processing.* Austin, TX: PRO-Ed.

Wagner, R., Torgesen, J., Rashotte, C. and Pearson, N. A. (2013) *Comprehensive Test of Phonological Processing (2nd edn) (CTOPP-2).* Oxford: Pearson Clinical.

Watson, J. E. and Johnston, R. S. (1998) *Accelerating Reading Attainment: The Effectiveness of Synthetic Phonics.* Interchange 57, SOEID, Edinburgh.

Wechsler, D. (2016) *Wechsler Intelligence Scale for Children (5th edn) (WISC-V).* Oxford: Pearson Clinical.

Wechsler, D. (2006) *Wechsler Individual Achievement Test (2nd edn) for Teachers (WIAT-II UK-T).* Oxford: Pearson Clinical. Available at www.psychcorp.co.uk/Education/Assessments/Achievement/WIAT-IIUKforTeachers(WIAT-IIUK-T)/WIAT-IIUKforTeachers(WIAT-IIUK-T).aspx, accessed on 14 September 2016.

Wechsler, D. and Naglieri, J. A. (2006) *Wechsler Nonverbal Scale of Ability (WNV).* Oxford: Pearson Clinical.

Weedon, C. (2016) 'The Potential Impact and Influence of the Social Model of Disability.' In L. Peer and G. Reid (eds) *Special Educational Needs: A Guide for Inclusive Practice* (2nd edn) (pp.63–76). London: Sage Publications.

Weedon, C. and Reid, G. (2004) *Special Needs Assessment Profile (SNAP V2 revised).* London: Hodder Murray.

Weedon, C. and Reid, G. (2008) *Special Needs Assessment Profile (SNAP V3).* London: Hodder Murray.

Weedon, C. and Reid, G. (2017) *Special Needs Assessment Profile – Revised (SNAP-R).* London: Hodder Education [in press].

Weedon, C. and Ruttle, K. (2012a) *Special Needs Assessment Profile (SNAP) Infant Check CD-ROM.* London: Hodder Education.

Weedon, C. and Ruttle, K. (2012b) *Special Needs Assessment Profile (SNAP) Infant Check User's Handbook.* London: Hodder Education.

Weedon, C., Reid, G. and Ruttle, K. (2017) *Special Needs Assessment Profile (SNAP V4).* London: Hodder/Rising Star.

Wendon, L. (1993) 'Literacy for early childhood: Learning from the learners.' *Early Child Development and Care 86,* 11–12.

Wilkinson, G. S. and Robertson, G. R. (2006) *Wide Range Achievement Test (4th edn) (WRAT 4).* Oxford: Pearson Clinical.

Willcutt, E. G. and Pennington, B. F. (2000) 'Comorbidity of reading disability and attention-deficit/hyperactivity disorder: Differences by gender and subtype.' *Journal of Learning Disabilities 33,* 2, March/April, 179–191.

Wiltshire County Council (2009) *Wiltshire Early Years SENCO Toolbox.* Trowbridge: Wiltshire County Council.

Wolfe, M. (2008) *Proust and the Squid.* Cambridge: Icon Books Ltd.

Wray, D. (2009) 'Extending literacy skills: Issues for practice.' In G. Reid (ed.) *The Routledge Dyslexia Companion.* London: Routledge.

Subject Index

Author Index

About the Author

Dr Gavin Reid is an international consultant and educational psychologist with consultancies in Canada, the UK, Europe, the Middle East, Asia and Australasia. He was visiting professor at the University of British Columbia (UBC) in Vancouver, Canada, in the Department of Education and Counseling Psychology and Special Education in 2007 and 2010.

He is chair of the British Dyslexia Association (BDA) Accreditation Board and an ambassador for the Helen Arkell Dyslexia Centre, and he is also an active consultant for the Child Enrichment Medical Centre in Dubai, the Centre for Child Evaluation and Teaching (CCET) in Kuwait and the Institute of Child Education and Psychology Europe (ICEPE).

Dr Reid is co-founder and director of the Red Rose School for children with specific learning difficulties in St Annes on Sea, Lancashire, UK, and visiting educational psychologist to organisations and schools in the UK, the Middle East, Asia and Egypt.

Dr Reid was formerly senior lecturer in the Department of Educational Studies (formally the Department of Special Education), Moray House School of Education, University of Edinburgh from 1991 to 2007, and wrote the first Master's course on Dyslexia in the UK in 1991.

Dr Reid has written 32 books on learning, motivation and dyslexia, and lectured to thousands of professionals and parents in over 80 countries. He has also had books published in Polish, Italian, Arabic, French, Greek and Slovak. One of his books, *Dyslexia – A Practitioner's Handbook,* is now in its 5th edition (Wiley/Blackwell 2016).

Dr Reid is also an experienced teacher with over 10 years' experience in the classroom, and has held external examiner appointments at 18 universities worldwide for PhD and Master's courses. He has been an active advocate for dyslexia being a key component of initial and post-graduate teacher training for many years.